Poker Essays, Volume III

By
Mason Malmuth.

A product of Two Plus Two Publishing

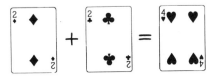

FIRST EDITION

SECOND PRINTING
MAY 2004

D0092092

Printing and Binding
Creel Printing Co.
Las Vegas, Nevada

Printed in the United States of America

POKER ESSAYS, VOLUME III
COPYRIGHT © 2001 Two Plus Two Publishing

For information contact: **Two Plus Two Publishing**
226 Garfield Dr.
Henderson NV 89074
(702) 896-1326

ISBN: 1-880685-27-2

Table of Contents

About Mason Malmuth

Mason Malmuth was born and raised in Coral Gables, Florida. In 1973 he received his BS in Mathematics from Virginia Tech, and completed their Masters' program in 1975. While working for the United States Census Bureau in 1978, Mason stopped overnight in Las Vegas while driving to his new assignment in California. He was immediately fascinated by the games, and gambling became his major interest.

After arriving in California, he discovered that poker was legal and began playing in some of the public cardrooms, as well as taking periodic trips to Las Vegas where he would play both poker and blackjack. In 1981 he went to work for the Northrop Corporation as a mathematician and moved to Los Angeles where he could conveniently pursue his interest in poker in the large public cardrooms in Gardena, Bell Gardens, and Commerce.

In 1983 his first article, "Card Domination — The Ultimate Blackjack Weapon," was published in *Gambling Times* magazine. In 1987 he left his job with the Northrop Corporation to begin a career as both a full-time gambler and a gambling writer. He has had over 500 articles published in various magazines and has authored or co-authored 14 books. These include *Gambling Theory and Other Topics,* where he tries to demonstrate why only a small number of people are highly successful at gambling. In this book he introduces the reader to the concept of "non-self weighting strategies" and explains why successful gambling is actually a balance of luck and skill. Other books he has co-authored are *Hold 'em Poker For Advanced Players,* written with David Sklansky, and *Seven-Card Stud For Advanced Players* written with David Sklansky and Ray Zee. All the "advanced" books are considered the definitive works on these games.

His company, Two Plus Two Publishing, has sold over 300,000 books and currently has 25 titles to its credit. These books are recognized as the best in their field and are thoroughly studied by those who take gambling seriously.

Other Books by Mason Malmth

Gambling Theory and Other Topics
Blackjack Essays
Poker Essays
Poker Essays, Volume II
Winning Concepts in Draw and Lowball

Gambling for a Living by David Sklansky and Mason Malmuth
Hold 'em Poker for Advanced Players by David Sklansky and Mason Malmuth
Seven-Card Stud for Advanced Players by David Sklansky, Mason Malmuth, and Ray Zee
The Professional Poker Dealer's Handbook by Dan Paymar, Donna Harris, and Mason Malmuth

Booklets with Mason Malmuth

Fundamentals of Craps by Mason Malmuth and Lynne Loomis
Fundamentals of Poker by Mason Malmuth and Lynne Loomis
Fundamentals of "21" by Mason Malmuth and Lynne Loomis
Fundamentals of Video Poker by Mason Malmuth and Lynne Loomis

Introduction

During the last twenty years I have spent my share of time at the poker tables. This includes working on my game and recognizing that poker is frequently a 24 hour a day occupation. Ironically, I'm not unhappy about this. Poker, in particular hold 'em and stud, can keep you busy virtually all the time. They are great games; they can be a lot of fun to play; and of course they can be quite profitable if you achieve expert status.

But there is another reason why this 24-hour-a-day activity is good. It means that poker is not simple. You see, if poker was easy, everyone would play it well; the game would be less interesting, and there would be no winners. Only luck would determine our short-term results, and only the "house" would be a long term winner. The myth of the professional poker player would be just that, a myth that those few who would even bother to play would simply laugh at.

Put another way, poker is a tough game and it needs to be a tough game. It takes dedication, study, and self control. Only a small number of people actually achieve expert status, and many who try fail.

There is also another aspect to poker that is rarely written about. This game will test your mettle. The reason for this is simple. Assuming you play well, your edge is relatively small when compared to the short-term luck factor. Circumstances will sometimes get out of control and you will see the worst brought out in many people.

This means you not only need to learn to play poker well, but must play well all the time. "Playing good" 90 percent of the time isn't enough. Only 100 percent will do.

Hence this book. It is the third collection of essays I have put together discussing the many aspects of poker. Most of the essays originally appeared as columns in *Poker Digest,* but some

1

2 Introduction

appeared elsewhere, including our web site at www.twoplustwo
.com and *Card Player* magazine.

   Sometimes the thoughts presented are very specific, such as
the particular playing strategies for a particular round in a
particular hand. Other times my thoughts are more general. This
includes my contempt for a few "pot limit players" and why you
should start small and work your way up striving to do better than
"minimum wage."

   In fact, one of the amazing characteristics about poker is that
many ideas which don't seem related, are in fact an integral part
of the game. This includes basic poker skills, judgement of others,
controlling your temperament, and how you interact with others
at the table. It all plays a role, and any lapses can be quite costly.

   With the above in mind, it is now time to enjoy the essays. If
I have done a good job, and you take this work seriously, your
game will improve. Hopefully you will benefit from my ideas.
And if this text accomplishes its purpose, it should contribute to
your 24-hour-a-day occupation.

   Finally, I would like to express my appreciation to Matty
Sklansky for editing this work. Thanks to him, my ideas are now
more clearly stated and thus should be more easily understood.

Part One
General Concepts

General Concepts

Introduction

Poker concepts can be classified into different groups. In one classification ideas apply to the play and results of all players. I call these "general concepts." However, even though the word "general" is used, the ideas can be very specific.

When playing poker and reading this book, your goal is to play the best you can, not to win the most money. Of course, always playing your best assumes that your long term results will allow you to win *your* maximum. But you usually won't be the biggest winner at the table — sometimes you will even lose — and there will always be a few people who seem to do better than you. This can be frustrating, but that's the way poker is. It can seem as if you are always "struggling to play good."

In fact, the first essay is "Struggling to be Good." Don't worry; you won't be the only one. In fact, all serious poker players constantly work to improve their game. This includes the best players, who may struggle the most.

This brings us back to the general concepts. In many ways I believe this to be the basic foundation of winning play. The following essays are just a sampling of the ideas contained in this area.

Struggling to be Good

I've been playing poker for many years now, and every so often I see the following pattern. A new player tries to make a name for himself at the hold 'em tables. Generally, this person is relatively young, somewhat intelligent, *believes* he understands the game better than virtually anyone else, but doesn't do very well. He can't understand why he doesn't do well, and often claims he is being cheated. But the fact is that his game still requires much development that only experience and the willingness to reevaluate his ideas will bring.

Of course he doesn't recognize this, but that's very often the way poker is. Specifically, many players who play quite poorly, think they play quite well. This is frequently the case in poker and is one of the reasons why limit games remain good over time.

Interestingly, when one of these players comes along his game usually follows the same pattern of those before him. The most common mistakes are as follows:

Mistake No.1: Stealing too much in late position. This is actually a symptom of being overly aggressive. Winning hold 'em requires that you pick up the blinds every now and then. But when the table is full you needn't be constantly attacking the blinds, due to the relatively small blind structure that hold 'em exhibits. Specifically, constantly attacking the blinds one to three positions off the button with hands like

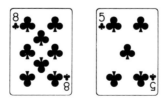

or

will prove to be very expensive.

I illustrate this by examining whom you may be against. Let's suppose the players in the blinds are loose. They should over defend. Thus you won't be picking up the blinds except when they have terrible hands. Furthermore, despite your advantageous position, you will frequently be holding the much weaker hand. Result: Your superior playing skills won't always overcome your disadvantage.

Now let's suppose the remaining players are tight. It wouldn't be so bad if this was their only characteristic, that is they are "weak tight." Unfortunately, many tight players also play quite well. This means that they should begin to pick up on what you are doing and they will adjust their play appropriately. You may find yourself being called more, reraised more, and having to face plenty of bets on the flop and beyond which will frequently be difficult to call because of the poor quality of your hand.

But there's another problem. Unless you are on the button, there will be players behind you, and when you raise they won't necessarily cooperate. (Now you may find yourself paying an extra bet and giving someone better hand and position over you. If he plays well, it's even worse.)

Mistake No. 2: Isolating weak playing opponents too much. This is another symptom of over aggressiveness. There is occasional value in isolating a weak opponent. You will have position on him, and even if your hand is only marginal, it may still be better than the holding of a weak, loose player. However, for this play to be profitable, you must be able to get heads up with your target. Too often attempting to isolate a weak opponent will frequently bring players in behind you, as well as the blinds. Furthermore, when the better players come in and/or the very aggressive ones, you may find yourself facing another bet. Now you will be the one out of position with the weak hand. Again, as above, you do not want to be giving players behind you better hand and position.

Mistake No. 3: Not understanding that some loose "gambling" opponents play better than you think. There is a class of hold 'em player who probably plays too many hands, but then plays his hands very well from the flop on. Most of these people do win, and a few of them do quite well. They are able to make up for their large hand selection through a good understanding of the strategic concepts that govern play on the flop and beyond, and through their hand reading skills. However, if you were to concentrate on their hand selection only, you may conclude that these players are not very good.

Generally, if you see someone playing too many hands, they don't play very well. This is especially true if they routinely call raises (in hold 'em) with hands like

But you must be aware that a small percentage of these people play much better than it appears.

When in a pot against one of these "many hands" selection experts you need to understand that your main advantage against them is that you tend to be playing with a little better hand. You also must understand that some of your starting advantage may be reduced as the hand proceeds. In other words, these are not the best players to attack. Most good players will usually stay away from them, recognizing that most of their earn comes from truly bad players, not from those who play a little too loose before the flop.

Mistake Number 4: Defending the big blind too much. We have already pointed out that our target player tends to attack the blinds with too many hands from the late positions. But this doesn't mean that everyone else does. Yet, many players with this characteristic tend to think that other players do the same thing. Thus, they defend their blinds too often.

There are two other reasons why they play too often in this spot. The first is that they do not always realize that the calling burden should be shared among all remaining players. Thus, the big blind should call far less in a three handed game when the player on the button raises, than he should in a two handed game (when the small blind is on the button). This is because there is a third person in the middle who should also do his share of calling (though not as much as the player in the big blind). This is true even though the pot will now be a little larger.

The second reason has to do with the fact that the raiser has position on you; therefore, is entitled to more of the pot than you are. Consequently, you can and should reduce your calling frequency a little from what the pot odds seem to indicate.

Of the several new players I see each year, my best estimate is that about one in five of these players actually matures into a successful poker player. More of them could accomplish this, but it seems their biggest stumbling block is their own personality. They just can't believe they don't know it all, and refuse to accept that fact that many of the more experienced players play more skillfully than they do.

What Happened
to the Lowball Stars?

In 1987 hold 'em and stud became legal in California, and the great poker explosion had begun. However, there was still plenty of poker in existence before this date. In fact, some of the super clubs such as the Bike and the Commerce were already open for business, with many poker games going all the time. However, only forms of draw poker were legal.

In case you didn't know, the most popular game was ace-to-five lowball draw played with a joker, which counted as the lowest card not already in your hand. My guess is that about two-thirds of the games in Southern California, where I lived in the early eighties, were lowball draw games. They came in all limits, from very small to the very large. I remember regularly seeing games at the $200-$400 level and higher. In addition, just like today, there were a few players who had become very well known because they were considered to be the best. They seemed invincible no matter what the limit, and no matter who their opponents were. But in a few short years after hold 'em was introduced, most of them were gone. They were unable to make the conversion from lowball draw to hold 'em, even though they were considered to be top poker players. So what happened?

I have contemplated this for years, and I believe these people went broke because lowball before the draw can look like hold 'em before the flop. Yet the two games are as different as night and day.

To see this, let's use $30-$60 limit as our model game. In lowball draw, we used to play it at an eight handed table with a $10 blind on the button, a $20 blind to the left of the button, and a $30 blind two positions to the left of the button. The first player in had the option to either fold, call the $30 blind, or raise an

9

additional $30. Also, all additional raises before the draw were in $30 increments.

$30-$60 hold 'em *appears* very similar. The game is usually nine handed instead of eight, and the $10 blind on the button is not adhered to, but everything else is the same. So it seemed like the old lowball stars could have moved to hold 'em with no problems. But they didn't. This new form of poker wasn't as easy as they thought and many players' bankrolls were destroyed.

The two primary differences unaccounted for were:

1.   Only two starting cards were dealt instead of five.
2.   There were four rounds of betting instead of two.

Consequently, the lowball players misplayed their hands and did not evaluate them correctly, particularly before the flop.[1]

To understand what happened, you first need to learn a little bit of correct lowball strategy before the draw. Opening play was very simple. If you were the first one to voluntarily put money in the pot you almost always raised. Occasionally someone would play a weak hand for a call, but they also might limp with a very strong hand. In either case, if you pretended that every pot was raised and based your playing strategy on this, you were on the right path.

So almost always raising if you were first in when playing lowball draw was clearly correct. You usually wanted to represent a completed hand because with five cards dealt to you that is what you could easily have. And with only two rounds of betting you were never very concerned with implied odds. (You also weren't concerned with other concepts, such as semi-bluffing, buying a free card, check raising, and the psychology aspect was not as sophisticated. But these ideas are not the thrust of this essay.)

───────────────

[1] In *Hold 'em Poker for Advanced Players* David Sklansky and I state that if you play your first two cards reasonably well and then only okay after that, don't expect to do much better than break even. However, if you play your first two cards poorly, your chances of being a winning player are quite small.

Hold 'em is a completely different animal. Hands vary widely in their initial strength. Some hands, such as ace-king, aren't as impacted by implied odds as hands like a medium suited connector or a small pair. In addition, a hand like

can frequently win without improvement if the number of players is kept small, while the other mentioned hands usually like many opponents. Plus, the community nature of hold 'em makes it difficult for certain hands to draw out against some other hands.

Thus, hold 'em requires a completely different strategy. Instead of raising every time when first in, you *should* do a lot of limping.[2] But even more important, a big distinction in playable hands is required depending on whether the pot is already raised or if someone has just called the big blind. In fact, if an opponent raises and you are next, the number of hands that you play should be far less than the number that you play if this same player had come in for the minimum. But in lowball it wouldn't matter much.

I believe that this was essentially the main problem. The lowball players didn't make this distinction. They thought that if a hand was playable against a limp, it must also be playable against a raise, and they were routinely calling raises with hands that should have been thrown away.

Specifically, a rough guideline in lowball was to call a raise with a hand that was as good as the original raiser's minimum raising hand. For example, if you somehow knew that an opponent's minimum raising hand in a certain situation was any four cards to a seven, you could play any four cards to a seven. On the other hand, if you somehow knew that an opponent's

---

[2] Except in very tight or tough games.

minimum raising hand in hold 'em was an ace-ten, you needed much better than an ace-ten to play. (Part of the reason for this is that hands like

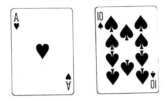

don't play very well against hands like

or against pairs that are tens or higher.)

So what happens if you adopt this lowball playing strategy to hold 'em? The answer is that you will lose your money fast. And I do mean fast. I believe that this is exactly what happened to many of the old time great California lowball players when the hold 'em revolution began.

Which Game: Stud or Hold 'em?

In most major cardrooms around the country, you usually have a choice between playing seven-card stud or Texas hold 'em, (and sometimes another form of poker). Generally, most players settle on one form or the other, and play nothing else. They either make their home at the stud tables, or find their way to the hold 'em side of the room... permanently.

Many new players aren't sure as to which game is better. If you live in the West or the South, you are most likely to become a hold 'em player, but if you live in the East, chances are you will be sitting at the stud tables. But the real question is, where should you try your luck? Assuming that you are new to poker, are you better off learning stud first, or is hold 'em a better choice?

(Before we go any further, I suggest that you eventually master both games if you are sincere about becoming a serious poker player. This is because they are both fun to play, and they both offer significant opportunities for the skilled player.)

It's turns out that the answer is fairly complicated, but like so many aspects of this great game, quite interesting as well. However, there are some rooms where you don't really have a choice. That is, only one form of poker is offered. For purposes of this discussion, we will assume that you do have a choice between stud and hold 'em.

Let's suppose you have enough money to play middle limit. I believe that against similar quality opposition the expert stud player can win a little bit more than the expert hold 'em player. This is due to more information available in stud; it's not because there is an extra betting round. It has more to do with the fact that there are upcards, and depending on the situation, stud hands tend to change value more than hold 'em hands. (It does takes longer to become an expert at stud, but that's another topic.)

However, in most of the cardrooms that I visit, and this is usually restricted to the cardrooms out west, the hold 'em games seem to be a little better. It appears that more new players who play poorly are coming into hold 'em than stud. This is probably because the "illusion of action" is greater in the flop games. At these limits more chips are usually on the hold 'em tables and the pots tend to be bigger.

I suspect that this statement is not completely accurate on the East Coast. Since stud is the predominant game, my guess is that both forms are getting their share of new players who are not at all skillful.

Now let's suppose you intend to be a small limit player. Here the choice is clearly hold 'em. As we will see later in this book, little stud is not the same as real stud. Real stud essentially begins at $15-$30 where the ante is finally large enough that you must play stud correctly. This means that you are constantly evaluating and re-evaluating your hands, and trying to knock people out. The smaller games are more of a trapping game which isn't the way stud is normally played, and it doesn't require standard seven-card stud skills. These small games are not the "crap shoot" that some people think. The tight player will get the money. Hence, since most small limit players want to become successful and eventually play higher, they should be playing hold 'em.

Of course you might argue that the small limit hold 'em games also play much differently from the higher limits. These games frequently feature many players who play too many hands and go too far with their hands. But even when this is the case, you still use most of the same concepts to make your decisions. It's just that these concepts frequently lead you to make different decisions than you would at the higher limits where the games are usually somewhat tighter.

If you have the bankroll to play the big limit games, stud is frequently the better choice.

To see why this is the case, you need to understand that poker requires a proper balance of luck and skill to be successful. The better players need to be reasonable winners at the end of the year.

This way they will return to start the games and keep them going. But there needs to be enough short term luck so that the weaker players will have some winning nights. This way they will also want to return. Unfortunately, as you move up in limit, the experts get even better, but a "live one" is usually a live one. Thus the games risk having the balance of luck and skill being tipped too much in favor of skill, which would mean that they could choke themselves off.

It turns out that high limit stud actually has a device to assure that this doesn't happen. It is what we refer to as a higher proportional ante. That is as you move up in limit at the stud tables, the ante becomes proportionately larger relative to the betting. This serves as a way to handicap the better players and assures that skill does not totally dominate luck.

Unfortunately hold 'em does not have a device of this sort. As you move up in limit the best players begin to dominate, and the weak players may discover that they lose their money at a rapid rate. For example, in a big cardroom, the highest hold 'em game that you might see could be a limit such as $40-$80, which might be next to a stud table where the stakes are five to ten times higher. Now I'm aware that few of us will be able to afford to play in these very high limit games, but if you do have such aspirations, you should probably focus on stud.

A Note on Steaming

Our company, Two Plus Two Publishing, has a web page located at www.twoplustwo.com. On this page we have several forums under the general heading "Theory and Strategy" which many of you participate in along with David Sklansky, Ray Zee, and myself. One of the most common questions is "How do you stop yourself from steaming?" A typical person will state, "I know how to play well, but when I get a couple of hands beat I start to play badly. I just can't help myself."

In fact, when playing poker I'm often asked this question by opponents who recognize me. They seem to think or hope that there are quick easy solutions to their psychological problems.

For many poker players this is an old problem. It's easy to play excellently when you are winning every pot. But when those pretty good hands get cracked, look out. At least this is the way it is for some would be experts, and if you are not careful, you can quickly lose what it takes a long time to win.

So how do you maintain the proper discipline that all players need to assure themselves of being winning players? I think I know the answer, and I'll bet my answer will surprise many of you. It is simply to make sure that you *understand* how to play extremely well.

Now "Wait a minute!" Some of you will say. "Isn't this a little double talk since the premise of this essay was that you do know how to play well?" I suspect that is not always the case. Over the years, I've met many self-proclaimed experts who eventually went broke or struggled to meet expenses. They would start to run badly and then steam their money away.

Take, for example, one particular expert player I have in mind who virtually never steams. He also plays great and understands everything that happens at the poker table. This includes sophisticated strategy to bad beats. So when something happens at the table that would be upsetting to many of you, he understands why it occurs, and goes on to the next hand. Furthermore, and this is very important, through his expert play he minimizes the amount of times that events go wrong. That's the key to his superb discipline.

And this brings up the point I want to make. I suspect that many steamers who claim they are playing well really aren't. And this lack of understanding is what makes them snap. It's not the bad beat they just suffered.

Here's an example. Suppose, when playing hold 'em, you are in an early position in a large multiway pot; you hold

and the flop is

You bet to avoid giving a free card, and five people call. The turn is a blank, you bet again for the same reason, and this time you get four callers. On the river another blank hits and you lose to someone who makes two little pair. You played your hand right but it caused you to go berserk.

(In fact, I hear these type of stories all the time. Someone plays his hand perfectly, it was the best hand all the way, but he never had a chance. It can seem like the world is against you and that you are destined to lose forever.)

Unfortunately, it turns out that you didn't play your hand right! This is because the size of the pot naturally draws lots of callers and you knew this. Furthermore, anyone with a small pair was correct to call due to all the bets in the center of the table. Thus you used strategy that was inaccurate for this particular situation (even though I know many players who will play it this way every time and argue that they are correct to do so).

In other words, I am asserting that many of you who have steaming problems are not playing as excellently as you think you are. The reason you steam is that you make frequent strategical errors that exacerbate your frustration. The solution is to do a lot more thinking about your game and any alternate strategies that may be available to you, and you must analyze all situations correctly.

There is an interesting aspect about poker which affects many players. It is simply that you can make many mistakes when playing and still be a winner. Other players who don't win will make even more errors than you.[3] Furthermore, you can frequently make the right play for the wrong reason. But if you don't understand the correct underlying strategy, you will eventually make some costly mistakes.

This is the precise category of player who is susceptible to steaming. When he learns to play better, the steaming will usually stop. If you fall into this category and can't recognize that your play needs some improvement, you may eventually steam most of your winnings away.

For example, many players will tell you that in loose games you must show down the best hand to win. While I agree that this statement is generally true, to be playing expertly you must be able to find that strategy which maximizes the chances that your hand is the best when the showdown comes.

So how do you overcome this problem? First you must recognize that you are a steamer. That's the first and perhaps most important step. Second, spend much more time thinking about the game, and make sure you think about the hands that you win as

---

[3] A few may make may make less errors but ones that are more costly.

well as those hands that drove you crazy. I'll bet that in time you will see that some of those hands you won could have been played much better. And third, watch those players who you know are highly successful and don't steam. If it appears that they play a hand differently from the way you would play it, you have something else to think about.

Examining the
Hand Rankings

In 1976, David Sklansky, a then unknown writer and young gambler, wrote a small book titled *Hold 'em Poker*. As many of you know, hold 'em has not been the same since. The hold 'em explosion had begun. One reason for this is that the text included a device called the "Sklansky Hand Groups." This was a "ranking of hands" which helped to quantify the starting hands and made it much simpler to understand. But it did more than just rank hands. It put some of the hands in the same Group because in many situations these hands could be played similarly.

Since that time, these rankings have gone through several changes. This has happened because the structure of the game has changed, and the players in general have become more knowledgeable and aggressive. However, these rankings are still subject to much debate. For instance, on our forum at www.twoplustwo.com, posters have discussed when ace-nine suited might be a better hand than king-queen off suit, even though the ace-nine suited is ranked lower than king-queen off suit. These are valid questions and the best players have a good understanding of the appropriate answers.

Changing the subject slightly, I'm now going to reveal a secret. When I play, I don't think in terms of the Sklansky Hand Groups. Neither does David Sklansky. We believe that it is an excellent device for someone new to the game, and if you are not an experienced player these hand groups should be memorized in order for you to become a winning player.[4] However, the best players usually think in terms of the intrinsic value of the hand for any particular situation. This is because the hands actually move

---

[4] It is not really necessary to memorize the rankings within a group however.

up and down the rankings depending on the number of players in the pot, your position, their position, how aggressive or passive the game is, how tight the blinds are, how well you and/or your opponents play after the flop, and so on. This is why in our book *Hold 'em Poker For Advanced Players* we give many examples where the hands actually change their presumed value, and if you wish to become a top player you will need to understand this.

To illustrate, I want to give two examples of hands which obviously flip-flop in the rankings. One is well known, while the other is fairly obscure.

The first compares jack-ten suited to ace-jack off suit. According to the rankings the suited hand is significantly higher — Group 3 versus Group 4. But suppose you were on the button and the player on your immediate right, who is first in, raises. Now you would prefer the ace-jack, even though we recommend that you reraise with both of these hands. The reason for this is that there are many situations where you will win with an ace high, but not with a jack high.

Now let's compare a pair of fives to eight-six suited. According to the rankings, these hands are about as close as you can get. They are each listed right next to each other in Group 6. Furthermore, let's suppose you are in a game where several players have limped in, and you are on the button. Of course you will play both hands, but which one would you rather have?

The answer will depend on how aggressive/passive the game is. If the game is aggressive, you prefer the pair. Now if you flop your set, you can expect many bets to go in the pot before the action gets to you and your implied odds would be gigantic. If the game is passive, you would prefer the suited connector. Now when you flop a weak draw, such as a gut-shot, you won't necessarily be bet out of the pot and may still be around if your miracle card comes, again increasing your implied odds. So you can see, even though these hands are listed right next to each other in the rankings, there can be a big difference in their value depending on the exact situation.

In conclusion, we can see that even though the Sklansky Hand Groups are a wonderful way to quantify the value of your starting hands, they are not set in concrete. As you become more experienced at hold 'em, you will see where it is proper to deviate from standard strategy, and also, where certain hands move up and down the rankings.

I do want to caution that creative players can sometimes move hands too far from their original ranking for their new evaluation to have much chance of being accurate. While understanding a hand's true intrinsic value for a given situation is important you shouldn't use this as an excuse to play a hand that only a "live one" would play. If you are not sure, it is usually better to err on the conservative side.

Pot-Limit Players

Sometimes when I'm playing in a middle limit hold 'em game, someone will sit down and announce that they are a "pot limit" player. They usually do this with a bit of sarcasm in their voice, as if to say us limit players are a little inferior since we don't have the courage to make a "big bet" and that we don't stand a chance against them.

I just love it when one of these announcements is made because these people lose virtually every time they are in my game. In fact, they usually lose their money quickly, get very mad, and leave in a huff. The fact is, these people generally have no understanding of limit hold 'em and stand little chance against even marginal players.

Years ago I wrote several columns as to why limit hold 'em is a strategically more difficult game than no-limit hold 'em. (See my book *Poker Essays* where these essays appear.) Many of the same comments would also apply when comparing limit hold 'em to its pot-limit cousin. When you cannot bet enough to protect your hand, you must frequently resort to other strategies which can be very tricky to execute correctly, and which very few people have mastered completely.

But that is not the thrust of this essay. It's purpose will be to discuss a couple of errors that these people make which forces them to lose their money very quickly in the limit form. (By the way, it's a shame they can't lose it a little slower. Then they wouldn't get mad and quit so fast, and would probably go through even more of their money.)

Their first mistake is to play too many hands. There is something about the size of the bet that makes them think that any two cards are frequently okay. In pot-limit, they are painfully aware that certain hands can trap you for a lot of money on a later street. What they seem to ignore in limit is that these same hands can also be very expensive, though not quite as much. Thus you see them playing any ace and other hands with questionable kickers; and they play them all the way through regardless of the action.

The next problem is that they always bet out and never understand what the size of the pot is. In pot-limit, since you can always bet the size of the pot, in a sense the pot is always the same size. This is not at all true in limit. For instance, sometimes when you bet you want anyone with a weak hand to call because they are not getting proper odds to do so — the pot is small; other times you want these same people to throw these exact same hands away — the pot is big.

This creates some tricky situations for the limit player. Sometimes the best play is not to bet what appears to be the best hand. It might be correct to go for a check raise, or it might be correct to play your hand passively on that round, and try to raise on the next round.

The third error that some of these pot-limit stars make is that they can turn into weak-tight players on the later rounds. In pot-limit the penalty for betting and being raised is greater than it is in limit play. Thus many pot limit players learn to always throw away marginal hands such as middle pair on the flop and fourth street, since against many opponents these hands can only beat a bluff (and you are getting poor pot odds to continue). In limit the opposite is true, not only do you need to call more because of the size of the pot compared to the bet, you should also be making more of these calls because your medium strength hand may beat some of the legitimate hands that your opponent might bet.

The last error worth discussing has already been mentioned. It is simply the fact that these "pot-limit" players refuse to accept the fact that to be good at limit hold 'em (or limit stud) you need to be a highly skilled poker player with a great knowledge of general poker concepts, as well as much specific knowledge that pertains solely to limit hold 'em. When you sit in a poker game and refuse to accept the fact that the game you are playing requires much skill to play at an expert level, that some of your opponents may be much more skillful than you are, and that you have a lot to learn about the game, you don't have a chance and should lose your money quickly. This, more than any other factor, is why these players usually leave the games mad after they have quickly lost part of their bankrolls. They just can't understand how these "simpletons" have ended up with their money.

Finally, I want to point out that there are a few people who are highly skilled at both forms of this game. The difference between them and our "pot limit" stars is that they worked very hard to achieve the skill levels that they have, and when they sit in a limit game you never hear them announce that they are "pot limit players." They are just there to do a job and do it the best they can.

Playing for Minimum Wage

If you are a new player, at what limit should you begin your play? I have always been an advocate of starting small and working your way up. That is, if you are new to poker, don't sit down in the medium or large games, which are frequently populated by the better players and, in general, there is no question that the players get better as you move up.

There are many other reasons why you should start out small. Most of them have to do with your initial development of poker skills, and some of these skills are ideas that very few of you have even thought about.

For instance, when you first begin to play poker what is the most important thing that you should do at the table? I believe that it is to hold your cards so that no one else can see them. Believe it or not, as simple and second nature as this is to all of us who have played for a while, it is something that first time players don't do very well. And this goes on top of the basic playing skills you need to learn.

I'm an example of what I recommend. The first time I played poker in a public cardroom was at the Lake Elsinore Casino in 1979 and the limit was $1-$2 (and the game was draw poker, jacks-or-better to open). But I didn't stay in these games long, and if your goal is to become a successful poker player neither should you (unless you just don't have the bankroll to move up).

There are several reasons for this. First, is that the skill level of many of your opponents is so low — remember, many of them are also new to the game — that it becomes somewhat difficult to master many of the skills necessary to manipulate opponents since they tend to be too loose to be tricked. Second, many of these games play very slowly because you are against people who play very slowly and are in virtually every pot. This takes a lot of the fun out of the game. And, third, mainly because of the limit and the slowness of the game, you just can't win very much. That is *don't expect to do much better than minimum wage.*

Let me give a specific example of what I am talking about. In the 21ˢᵗ Century Edition of our book *Hold'em Poker for Advanced Players* David Sklansky and I state the following in the loose games section:

"It's so important to increase your chance to win the pot that it can be right to bet a hand that you know is beat. For instance, if you have

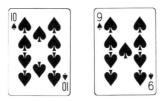

the flop comes

and the pot is pretty big, it is almost mandatory to bet if you are in early position. You do this not only because you might make a straight, but because it is important to get hands like

or

out. You would bet even if you knew that someone had a six or a seven in their hand and was going to call you all the way. If a nine or a ten comes on the river you want to maximize your chance of winning. (You should be even more inclined to bet if you have a backdoor flush draw as well.)"

Thus, your bet should increase your chances of winning the pot by a little bit, and in a very large pot this risk-reward ratio is well worth it. (For those of you who are questioning this play, keep in mind that even in a large multi-way pot no one has to have an ace.)

The reason I mention this play is that on our forum at www.twoplustwo.com there has been much discussion concerning it. Many people have said that in the games they play, the hands that we are trying to fold out just won't get out, and sometimes players holding these hands will even call raises cold. Therefore this bet is costing you money. Are they right?

It turns out that there are probably a few games around the country where many players will automatically call this bet regardless of their holding. They just see a big pot and throw the money in no matter how foolish their call might be. But these calls can hurt you if you are trying to play as we describe.

So where do these games occur? They generally show up at the smallest limits in a cardroom that is located in an area that has a large population, or at a cardroom which has just opened and poker is new. So here our advice may be a little too sophisticated for the game. But the above mentioned problems arise. You won't do much better than minimum wage, and we don't write for people who are just interested in making minimum wage.

So what's the conclusion? Do what I did. Start in the smallest limits to get your feet wet and to learn basic poker skills. But as soon as you can, try to get out of those $1-$2 and $2-$4 games. In Las Vegas, which I call home there are plenty of $6-$12 and $8-$16 games where you can begin to make some real money. These games are not filled with experts, and they are frequently very good. But many of the concepts we talk about, do begin to apply. You should find similar conditions in many cardrooms throughout the country and if you study hard and get the proper playing experience, you should begin to do better than minimum wage.

To finish, I want to address some of my critics who claim that since I only play in tough "Las Vegas" games, I don't really have a good conception as to what some of these other games are like. Well it turns out that I played in what were probably the best hold 'em games that ever existed. These games occurred in June of 1987 which was the first month that stud and hold 'em were legal in California. I spent most of my time at the clubs in Gardena and in many cases I was the only one sitting at my table who had any idea what proper strategy was.

Drawing to the Ignorant End

One bit of advice which I have heard for years and years, and seen literally hundreds of times in print is not to draw to the ignorant end. What this means is that in a limit hold 'em game if you have the bottom end of a straight draw and can make your hand without making the nuts, your cards should hit the muck. The idea is that you don't want to complete your straight when someone else makes a better hand.

Well I agree that you don't want to make your hand when someone else makes a better hand, but in limit hold 'em, where the pot commonly gets large relative to the size of the bet, this is a chance that you should frequently take. Of course you don't do this when your hand has virtually no chance of being good. For instance, if the flop came

and you hold the

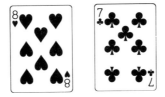

you shouldn't be calling trying to make a pair.

But what if the flop is something like

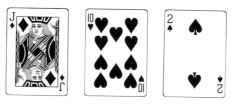

and you hold the

Notice that if you call, you will be drawing to the ignorant end. You could catch a queen and lose to an ace-king or a king-nine since both of these hands would produce higher straights than yours. On the other hand, if neither of these holdings is out, you may win several double size bets if the queen comes. You will also have the nuts if a seven comes, and given the two card gap that the seven will produce, your hand can be very deceptive, which will increase your profits even more.

One way to see that this call is correct is that in many situations the pot will be big enough or almost big enough to call for the purpose of catching only the seven. For instance, if there are seven or eight bets in the pot, you should play even though it is approximately an 11-to-1 shot to make the nuts since you expect to collect extra bets if the miracle card does appear. Now if you chose to make this call in a moderately large pot but were also prepared to fold if the queen came and someone else bet you would still show a profit.

Furthermore, depending on the action, there should be many times where it will be obvious that your hand is good if the queen does come. (Those other hands don't have to always be there.) In these spots you can always bet for profit and collect what is in the pot plus some additional money from whoever calls you down.

This means that you certainly don't need a pot large enough to justify drawing to the one card — the seven — only. In fact, though it is not the purpose of this essay, there are many spots where you would take the lead with this hand by either betting or raising.

Now let's suppose you hold a hand like

and the flop comes

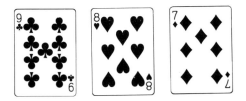

Observe again that you are drawing to the ignorant end. But this time the situation is very different.

First, notice that a straight can already be out there, and if so, the best thing that can now happen is that you split the pot when your straight card comes. (A five will give you a split against a six-five, and a ten will give you a split against a ten-six.) But if an opponent holds a jack-ten, you are drawing dead.

Second, notice that if a ten comes and you are against several players it is fairly unlikely that your hand will be good, since anyone with a jack beats you. And third, if a five comes, you may like your hand a little better, but it is not the nuts and you could easily be splitting the pot if anyone else also holds a six.

(In the previous example it is much harder to split the pot since someone else would have to hold two cards which are the same ranks as your two cards. But in this spot, they only need one card, the six in this case, to match.)

So here, drawing to the ignorant end is usually a mistake. There are a few exceptions (see below), but if your strategy was to always throw hands like this away, you wouldn't be off by much.

However, there is one exception that I want to mention. In a short-handed pot, you may want to bet the bottom end of a straight draw in an attempt to steal the pot if no one else has yet bet. Now someone who has a hand like middle or bottom pair may fold, and you want him to do so. Nonetheless, if called, you may still win by making a straight. Against most players, this "semi-bluff" should show a profit.

In conclusion, I hope this essay resolves the confusion about drawing to the ignorant end. Now the next time you hear it, you'll know exactly what the correct strategy is. By the way, you'll usually hear it when taking down the pot as your opponent will question why you would make such a play.

Those Marginal Hands Again

For years I have warned against using computer simulations which draw too many conclusions about how a poker hand should be played. Seeing how a certain hand does against some number of opponents who hold random cards is not a good model for poker, and does not require much discussion. I believe that virtually everyone who reads this will quickly agree.

Today there is good news and bad news. The good news is that the poker simulators are much better. It appears they do a pretty good job of playing poker. All you need to do is pick a particular hand, play it against some particular line-up of players, and your results will determine your strategy. The bad news is that these results can be very dangerous.

For example: Suppose you are under-the-gun in a hold 'em game and are dealt ace-jack offsuit. Should you play this hand? This topic has been hotly debated on our Internet forums. Some think it should always be played, others say rarely. And some, such as myself, come down in between.

One thing is for certain. It is a marginal hand. When it should be played upfront, assuming you play it well, it won't show much long term profit.

So what do the simulations show? According to one of our posters, they clearly show the hand to be profitable in virtually all situations. Thus, he has concluded that ace-jack offsuit should always be played in this spot.

However, I question the accuracy of the simulators. Another poster stated that one of the more popular of these programs didn't take into account the position of the raiser. If that's the case, it may over value some hands a little bit and under value others because the person who gets to act last has a positional advantage.

In fact, I believe that this is the problem. My guess is that the simulators may have enough errors in them that in some cases their inherent errors may be larger than the differences they are trying to measure. Thus, they may determine that a hand is slightly profitable, when in reality, it is not.

"So what?" "What's the big deal if I play a hand that I think is slightly profitable but it turns out my statistical measure is off a little bit? How can this make much difference in the long run?"

Well, if your game was seven-card stud, I would agree. You would be holding a marginal hand and if you played it every time it would have very little effect on your long run expectation. But hold 'em is a different animal.

You see, in hold 'em everyone has the same board. In games like stud (or draw poker) the hands are roughly statistically independent of each other. Of course this isn't completely true, but in flop games everyone has the same five cards in the center of the table. What I believe this means is that hold 'em contains far less marginal hands than other forms of poker.

In my book, *Poker Essays,* there is a chapter entitled "Marginal Hands." In it I talk about hands which tend to be either slightly profitable or very unprofitable, but you can't be sure which. Obviously, when this is the case, you should throw it away.

Suppose you have that ace-jack offsuit, are under-the-gun, but are in a tough game that features several players who can use their position to great advantage, and who are capable of making sophisticated plays. It should be obvious that your hand is now either a small winner or a big loser, and you should quickly throw it in the muck no matter what the simulations might indicate.

Five Skills to Work On

If you are new to poker but are taking the game seriously you may have noticed that it is much more complex than you first thought. This is because to become a top player there are a large number of skills that you must master. Put another way, there is no "magic bullet." There isn't just one thing that you can concentrate on and expect to win lots of money.

This happens to be good news if your goal is to become an expert. Remember, as stated in the "Introduction" to this book, if poker was easy everyone would master it and there would be no winners.

However, for the purposes of becoming a top player I have picked out five skills which you will need to become completely proficient at. They are:

1.   Hand Selection
2.   Check Raising
3.   Reading Hands
4.   Semi-bluffing
5.   The Ability to Vary Your Game

Ironically, if you are playing low limit poker and are against many opponents who play too many hands and go too far with their hands, not all of these skills will seem important. Nevertheless, if you have hopes of moving up in limit where you can make some real money, they are absolutely essential to winning play.

Again I want to state that there are many other skills which top players possess and use to make extra money. But if you master the above five, that, you will be well on your way to a successful poker career, and you will discover that many of the other poker skills will come fairly easily.

The five skills are discussed in more detail below.

Skill No.1: Hand Selection. Selecting the right hands to play and knowing the correct way to play them is obviously essential for winning play. Typical players play too many, and a few rocks actually don't play enough. However, very few people actually play all hands dealt to them correctly (and this includes throwing them away). The real key to hand selection is to understand the precise value of the particular hand for the particular situation that you are in. This value is influenced by your position, the number of players already in, whether the pot has been raised, how well your opponents play, and the fact that poker is a seven-card game. Also, as the examples will show, evaluating stud hands is more difficult than evaluating hands while sitting at the hold 'em table. This is due to the fact that in stud there are upcards and that stud hands are usually more sensitive to the number of players in the pot than their hold 'em counterparts.

Here are a two examples from hold 'em.
1. We are all aware that a pair of aces is always a good hand, but what about a hand like

It varies from fairly strong to very weak. It would be considered fairly strong if you are first in from a late position. Your raise may allow you to win the pot without a fight, and if you are called, you may win without improving. On the other hand, you would certainly not want to call an early position raiser if you were sitting on his immediate left. If he doesn't have you badly beaten, there could easily be a player behind you who does.
2. A pair of deuces is a better hand than ace-king if only two cards were dealt, however the seven-card nature of hold 'em

make the ace-king far superior. Ace-king is almost equivalent to two deuces without improvement, but is about three times more likely to improve.

Here are two examples from seven-card stud.

1. Three flushes are greatly influenced by the cards that are out. Most everyone knows this. You don't want to be calling a third street raise if several of your suit are present in the upcards of other player's hands. But what most people don't know is that the individual cards that make up your three flush can often impact the correct way to play your hand. For example, if you also hold a live ace, and you are playing in a game where the ante is moderately large — this usually means $15-$30 and above — you may want to raise or reraise if you can get the pot heads-up.

2. Calling with the worst pair can easily be correct if you feel that it is likely that your opponent's probable pair is dead and you have a straight flush kicker. For example, suppose you have:

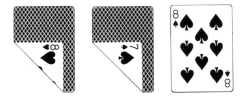

Your opponent raises with an ace up, you feel that he likely has aces, but another ace is out, and your hand is completely live. The correct play is for you to call, and sometimes even reraise, if that is what it takes to get heads up. (This again assumes that you are in a game where the ante is at least moderately large.) If your hand was not completely live, or no other ace was showing, you should probably fold. (By the way, this is an example of some of the complexity that exists in stud which is not present in hold 'em. Upcards do make a difference.)

Skill No. 2: Check Raising. Check raising is checking your hand with the intention of raising on the same round after an opponent bets. The two standard reasons for check raising are to either get more money into the pot or to knock other players out. When most people check raise they are usually trying to accomplish the first of these goals, but in many situations trying to knock other players out is much more important. This usually occurs when the pot is very large and you feel that most players will simply call your bet and frequently be right to do so (because of the size of the pot). But they won't necessarily call two bets.

Here are a two examples from hold 'em.

1. Let's start with a standard example. You are in an early position with a hand like

and the flop comes queen high. The pot is short handed; and after you limped in before the flop, you were raised by a loose-aggressive player (or perhaps you called his raise out of the blind). Since you are very sure that he will bet automatically, you should strongly consider check raising. It's true that there is some chance you will run into a better hand, or that he will call and draw out on you whereas your bet would have made him fold, but given his characteristics for raising with many hands (before the flop), you have a fairly automatic play where you want to get more money in the pot.

2. Here's a more unusual example. Suppose several people just
    limp in and you hold a medium large pair in the small blind
    such as

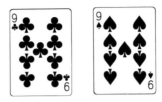

You call and the flop is

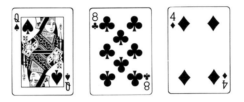

Even though you think that there is some chance you have
the best hand you decide to check and make a decision
depending on the action. If there is a bet and a raise you will
fold. If there is a bet and a couple of callers you will also
fold. But suppose the bet comes from a late position player
and no one else is in. A check raise may be the appropriate
strategy.

This play would become correct if:

A. You are against opponents who would have not checked
    a queen since they do not like to give a free card.
B. The late position player is aggressive and would
    automatically bet a hand like middle pair or a gut shot
    draw as well as a queen.

If this is the case, a check raise to knock players out becomes
mandatory, because you cannot afford to let other players in
who have overcards to your pair. Given the size of the pot
and the chances that you currently have the best hand, calling

is clearly inferior to raising; even though you might be raising with the second best hand.

Here are two examples from seven-card stud.

1. You limp in on third street with a live three flush. The player on your immediate left raises with the highest card on board. Given his position and the other upcards, it appears likely that he has a big pair. Two other players call and you also call. On fourth street you make a four flush by catching a bigger card than he has showing, and all other players (including the original raiser) catch blanks. For example, suppose on fourth street your hand is:

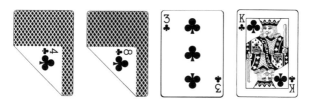

while his hand is:

You know that if you bet, your scary board will cause everyone to just call. But if you check, the third street raiser will probably bet again; the other players may call, and then you can check raise to get more money in the pot. By the way, even if the other players both fold, you would still probably want to check raise because a four flush with an overcard on fourth street is a favorite against a lone pair.

2. Now suppose you are against the same three players and everyone has the exact same hands, but this time after you limped in the raiser is last. That is, you limped, two other players limped, and then the player with the Q♦ in the door raised. On fourth street the cards are the same. Now you are first to act and the third street raiser is last. Again, you may want to go for a check raise if you are fairly sure that the other two players will check and the third street raiser will bet. (If not, you should bet yourself.) This way if you pair your king, your chances of winning go up since you will be against one player instead of three.

    Notice that something very unusual has happened here. In the first (stud) example we wanted to check raise to get more money in the pot, and in this example, where all players have the exact same hands, we want to check raise to knock them out. As you can see, the difference is your position relative to the other players. That is, even though your cards are important, when making these decisions there are other parameters to think about, and the best players do a good job of evaluating and incorporating these other parameters into their decisions.

Skill No. 3: Reading Hands. This is one of those skills, that in many low limit games, where many of your opponents are playing loose and wildly, that does not seem to be very important. This is because bad players are apt to play anything. However, as you move up in limit, this changes, and there is no doubt that reading hands is the major separator between the merely good players and the great players.

Reading hands is the science of figuring out exactly what your opponent holds. Generally, the most common way to read hands is to analyze the meaning of an opponent's check, bet, or raise, and then to consider the plays he has made throughout the hand, along with the exposed cards, to come to a determination about his hand.

Being able to accurately put an opponent on his correct hand has tremendous value. To see this, imagine what it would be like to play if your opponent always turned all his cards face up. You would be able to get extra bets in, save money when you are beat, and would never play a hand in a less than optimal fashion. As you can see, having this ability is a great asset, and it is most easily realized against players who will play their hands in a straight forward, rational manner.

Here are two examples from hold 'em.
1.   I'll start with a simple example. Suppose you hold

in an early position, and a tight, unimaginative player on your right opens with a raise. You should fold. The reason is based, mainly, on the hands that he will play (plus the fact that you can run into a better hand behind you). So what hands will he play for an opening raise? It will usually be aces, kings, queens, jacks, ace-king, or ace-queen. If you look at this list, you should quickly see that even though you hold a good hand, you will not be in good shape most of the time. Thus you should fold.[5]

Now suppose the situation is the same but your opponent instead of being tight and unimaginative, fits the loose-aggressive category. Now, in addition to the list above your opponent will raise with many more pairs, hands like ace-jack, ace-ten, ace-little suited, king-queen, king-jack, queen-

---

[5] A good discussion of this concept appears in John Feeney's book *Inside the Poker Mind*. See the chapter titled "Do You Pass the Ace-Queen Test?"

jack suited, and so on; and even occasionally raise with a hand like seven-six suited. Throwing your hand away is now a mistake. In fact, just calling is also a mistake. You should reraise every time in this situation.

2. Here's a more complex example that actually occurred in a game that I played in the other night. In a multiway pot I held

good hand reading ex.

in the big blind. The pot was not raised, and because of my poor position, the fact that my raise wouldn't knock anyone out and the fact that there was a tight-solid player who had limped in under the gun, I also decided not to raise. The flop came:

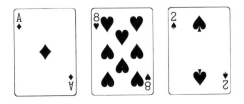

I bet, and before the solid player could act, a wild player, on his immediate left, raised out of turn. The solid player then put his (one) bet into the pot knowing that it was going to at least two bets. I then made it three bets, and the solid player made it four bets. So what is his hand? It almost has to be a set of eights. First he would not play a hand like ace-eight or ace-deuce suited (or not suited) right up front. Second, he might call the raise with a holding like ace-jack, but he certainly would *not* make it four bets. And third, he wouldn't play a small pair under the gun. This only leaves one hand,

which must be a pair of eights. I immediately threw my
A♠K♥ away.

Here are a couple of examples from seven-card stud.

1. Those of you familiar with stud know that it is very
dangerous when your opponent pairs his doorcard. When this
happens on the early rounds, you are forced to give up on
some good hands (unless you want to lose your money).

   Let's suppose you open with a raise and you hold a pair
of kings with a king up. You are called by a couple of
players, including one who plays fairly well. On fourth street
you catch a blank, but the opponent in question pairs his
doorcard. Normally you should fold. But if you remember
that another card of his rank was also out on third street you
can consider calling. In addition, if you remember that his
suit is also live, you would definitely call. This is because his
chances of having three-of-a-kind have gone down, and it is
much more likely that all he has is a pair and a three flush.

2. Our second example is much more sophisticated. Suppose
after several people have limped in a very good player raises
with a J♠ up. You suspect that he only has a pair of jacks
because you know that he is aware that a pair of jacks, while
being a good starting hand, loses value against several
opponents. On sixth street his hand looks like

and he has bet on every street into several players. What
might he have? One possible answer is a pair of jacks with a
four flush. For the same reason that you will raise many
limpers with a hand like ace-jack suited at hold 'em, but only
call if your hand is not suited, it makes sense to raise several

players in stud with a hand like a pair of jacks *and a straight flush kicker,* but to only call if your kicker is poor. Since this player has caught two hearts and keeps betting into several players, don't be surprised to if he has something like

in the hole. Thus, if he bets again on the river and you make a straight, it may be better to only call, even if you are absolutely sure that he started with a pair of jacks.

Skill No. 4: Semi-bluffing. In the *Theory of Poker*, David Sklansky defines a semi-bluff as "a bet with a hand which, if called, does not figure to be the best hand at the moment, but has a reasonable chance of outdrawing those hands that initially called it." A semi-bluff can only occur when there are more cards to come, and when you make this bet, you are hoping to win the pot right there. However, if you are called, you still have some chance to win the money.

Semi-bluffing can add much deception to your game. If you never bluff, your game is too predictable, and the better players will easily figure out your holdings. When you do bluff, there are many situations where a pure bluff won't be worth it, but a semi-bluff will, since it is the combination that your opponent folds, plus your chances of making a winning hand that show a profit. There are no successful players at either stud or hold 'em who do not understand semi-bluffing. To become successful, this is one skill you can't ignore.

Here are a two examples from hold 'em.
1.   Suppose you hold:

in the big blind, and a couple of players have limped in. The flop is:

You bet. Notice that you hold bottom pair with an over card. If no one else has a pair, you might win on the spot. If someone else holds a trey, even if they have a better kicker, they still might fold. Even if someone has a seven, giving him middle pair, he may also fold, especially if there is a player to act behind him. If someone plays against you and they hold a better hand, you still may win if either a queen or another trey hits the board.

2. Before the flop you are first in, and raise with:

You get a couple of callers and the flop comes:

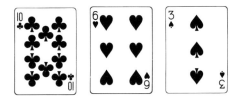

All you have are two overcards, a three flush, and a (bad) three straight. You bet, but are raised by one of your opponents. You figure him for top pair; you call, and the two of you see the turn card which is the

Now your hand is much better. In addition to your overcards, you have a draw at the nut flush. Thus, if your opponent is not sharing one of your cards, you may have as many as 15 outs. Against the right player, you go for a semi-bluff raise. Although checking and calling will show a profit, given the size of the pot, it may be right to invest the extra money, if your opponent will also occasionally fold. In other words, checking and raising may be an even more profitable strategy. (By the way, if you do make this semi-bluff raise and get called, and a blank now hits on the river, it is usually right to bluff again since there are some players who will decide to call your raise, but then fold if they don't improve.) One final caution. Even though this play is profitable against the right player, it is still expensive when it fails. So pick your victims carefully.

Here are two examples from seven-card stud.

1. Again we start with a simple example. On third street, you are high with an ace, and have a king and a ten in the hole. An early position player raises with a ten up, and you figure his most likely hand is a pair of tens. If your ace and king are live, and no one else is in, you may want to reraise as a semi-bluff.

    Assuming you both go to the river, depending on the other upcards and your opponent's kicker, you may only win as little as 35 percent of the time, which is not often enough to make a call profitable, assuming typical action. But your semi-bluff raise can change that. Now your opponent may fold immediately. He may also fold if you catch a small pair showing by fifth or sixth street. Furthermore, if you don't improve, and check on a later street, he may also check, fearing an over pair, and be glad that you gave him a free card (when in actuality he is the one giving you the free card). As you can see, the semi-bluff raise can help your hand in many ways.

2. You start with a three flush in a multiway pot that has been raised by a player with a king up. On fourth street you catch what appears to be a blank, but actually make a small pair. The player with the king bets again and you call. On fifth street you catch an offsuit ace which is live. The player with the king has now caught two non-threatening cards. You may want to try for a checkraise semi-bluff.

    First, notice that your hand is now good enough to chase to the river since you have a pair, an ace, and a three flush against a likely pair of kings. But if your raise makes your opponent think that you might have made aces up he may fold which is a giant gain for you. If called, however, you have many ways to win — this includes two small pair against unimproved kings or possibly backdooring a flush on the final two cards, as well as improving to aces-up or three-of-a-kind (or better).

Skill No. 5: The ability to vary your game. When playing poker, if you fall into certain playing patterns, it will be easy for your more observant and knowledgeable opponents to take advantage of this. For example there is one player who I play against fairly regularly who almost always tries to check raise if he flops top pair or better, but will always lead with a flush draw. Needless to say this is something I take advantage of.

Here are a two examples from hold 'em.

1.   Suppose you hold

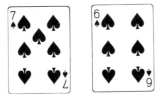

are in early position, and no one else has voluntarily put money in the pot. Against observant opponents, particularly if the players in the blind are tight or are aware that you will "only" raise with a high quality hand up front, you should occasionally go ahead and raise. My recommendation is that you raise with a hand like this, providing the situation is right, approximately 20 percent of the time.[6] (You would usually fold the rest of the time.)

Here's what can happen. First you might steal the blinds. Second, you might be able to steal on the flop or a later street. And third, you might make something, get called down, win a nice pot, and totally confuse your opponents. By the way, if you do win the pot without a showdown, I

---

[6] "Providing the situation is right" is extremely important when deciding to make this play. It also means that in general you should raise with a hand like this far less than "20 percent of the time."

recommend that you keep your hand to yourself. This will allow you to make the play again.

2.   Here's a play that's a little more complicated. Suppose you raise before the flop with a hand like:

and are called by only one player who acts before you. Perhaps the person in the big blind or perhaps someone who limped in before you. Now the flop comes something like:

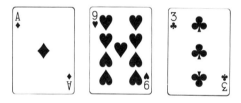

It looks like you have flopped a powerhouse hand, but to your surprise, your opponent bets into you. When this happens you must realize that your opponent either has you badly beat, perhaps he flopped a set or a hand like top two pair, or you have him badly beat; perhaps he also has an ace with a weaker kicker, or is on a total bluff.

When this is the case, a little deception may be called for. Most players in this situation will raise on the flop, thinking they have the best hand, wanting to get more money in the pot. However, if they don't have the best hand, that raise will cost them money. In addition, if the bettor is bluffing, the raise can also be expensive in the sense that your opponent will now fold, costing you additional bets.

An alternative strategy is to simply call your opponent down and possibly raise on the river. Not only will you gain extra money if your opponent has the weaker hand, but many players will remember this play and be reluctant to value bet into you in other situations.

As for stud, I'm not going to give any specific examples, because in stud your hands can change value so dramatically that playing them non-deceptively can appear to many players that you are in fact being tricky. We have much discussion of this in the 21st Century edition of our book *Seven-Card Stud for Advanced Players.*

It turns out that there are two aspects of seven-card stud that most hold 'em players are not used to, and that many stud players do not handle well. They are the fact that upcards are present, and the fact that stud hands are much more sensitive to the number of people in the pot as long as you are playing in a game where the ante is relatively large — this usually means $15-$30 and higher. The fact is that many hands such as pairs, three high cards, and three flushes that contain a high card such as an ace or a king prefer to be heads-up.

Suppose you are dealt

and a player with a queen up raises. What is the correct play?

My guess is that most players will say to reraise, and in many situations this would be the proper strategy. But let's suppose that after the queen raised two other players called. One of your kings is out, and you are last to act before the bring-in, so you can't knock anyone out behind you (except of course the bring-in who probably won't play anyway). Notice that in this situation your hand has lost much of it's value. You should still play, but a raise is not called for.

But what else have you accomplished by not raising? It will appear to many of your more observant, but less sophisticated, opponents that you decided to play your hand with deception. They won't realize that you didn't raise because your hand lost much of it's value. To them, you had the best hand, and varied your play. Now the next time you call with a king up, they won't be sure what you have, and they might misplay their hand.

Why Stud
Players Lose at Hold 'em

On one of our forums, a poster pointed out that when good stud players sit in his regular hold 'em game, they don't seem to do very well. I have also noticed this; and in addition; have observed that good hold 'em players frequently do poorly at seven-card stud.

To the uneducated eye, these games can look very similar. In fact, on many occasions I've been told that Texas hold 'em is a form of seven-card stud. But there is no question that the proper strategy for each game is very different, and there are very few players who excel at both. So what follows are four reasons and some explanations as to why stud players do poorly at hold 'em. In the next essay, we'll reverse the process and look at why hold 'em players do poorly at stud.

Reason No. 1: There is less independence between hold 'em hands. Because hold 'em is a community board game — that is the up cards in the center of the table are in everyone's hand — it makes it much easier for second best hands to appear. For example, normally a hand like

is a strong starting hand. But if you happen to be against someone holding ace-king and an ace flops, it can be quite expensive. Your hand will usually appear too strong to get away from, yet you will have very little chance of drawing out.

Because of this (and some other reasons) good stud players tend to play more starting hands than good hold 'em players. If they do this, they are more likely to get trapped when playing hold 'em situations which have lost much of their value because their potential to make something second best has gone way up.

Reason No. 2: It is more difficult to draw out with one pair hands. This is actually a special case of the hands being less independent. In stud, many of your wins occur because you take a small pair up against a large pair and make two pair while the hand with the large pair doesn't improve. At the hold 'em table this is less likely to happen because of the community cards in the center of the table. Now if a pair appears on board, it has entered the hands of both players and the hand that began best, will stay best.

This means that it is not correct to chase as often when heads up in hold 'em as it is in stud. There are many situations in stud, such as when you have a small pair, an overcard kicker, and your hand is live, going to the river against someone with a likely big pair is almost automatic. (The main exception is when they make something threatening on board.) This is not the case in hold 'em, and routinely calling in these situations, which many stud players do, will prove very expensive.

Reason No. 3: Calling on the flop and the turn is not as automatic as calling on fourth and sixth street. Many stud players believe that fifth street is where you should be releasing your hand if it has not sufficiently improved. This is because, on this round of betting, the limit doubles, and by calling, you may trap yourself for three (or more) double size bets. Of course there are exceptions, but this strategy is very often correct. Many hands that you play on third street can afford the small fourth street bet, and if you call on fifth street, calling on the next round is frequently automatic.

Here's a simple example. Suppose you start with a small three flush such as

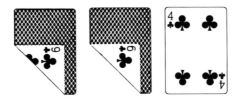

On fourth street you catch a large card such as a king or an ace, it is live, and it appears that the bettor has a pair of queens. Your hand has improved enough for you to call. But on fifth street you will frequently fold unless your hand improves.

In hold 'em, there just aren't equivalent plays. Sometimes you will call with weak hands such as a gut shot or bottom pair on the flop, but this would only be correct if the pot is very large and/or there are many players to collect from in case you get lucky and hit your hand.

The same is true on the turn. It is not like sixth street in stud where the call is fairly automatic. I won't give any examples, but there are many hold 'em hands that should quickly be abandoned here, even though they were correct to play for one bet on the flop.

Reason No. 4: The river can be played more accurately in hold 'em. One aspect of stud that makes the game very different is that the last card is dealt face down for everyone. In hold 'em, since the river is dealt face up in the center of the table, you not only get to see your card, but you get to see everyone's else's as well. This means that the expert hold 'em player can make some very extreme plays. He can sometimes throw away a really good hand, but conversely often bet a marginal hand for value. Stud players tend to play the last round much more cautiously. They value bet less, and payoff more. While this approach is frequently correct when playing seven-card stud, it can prove somewhat expensive in the long term when playing hold 'em.

Here's a simple example. Sometimes, when playing either hold 'em or stud, you can be virtually certain that your opponent is on a flush draw. Now, if the flush card comes on the river, you can fold at the hold 'em table. The stud player frequently pays off because one cannot see whether the opponent's last card was of the appropriate suit. In addition, the hold 'em expert might be able to make a "value-bet" on the end if the flush card does not get there — the river card might pair his opponent who will now pay off. In stud the expert will frequently just be in a check and call mode.

Why Hold 'em
Players Lose at Stud

In the previous essay we looked at why good stud players frequently do poorly at hold 'em. This time we will turn it around and examine why good hold 'em players don't always fare that well when they sit down at the stud table. However, that being said, I believe that hold 'em players who don't fully understand stud actually have a little better chance than stud players who don't fully understand hold 'em. This may seem surprising since I also believe that stud is a more difficult game to play at an expert level than hold 'em. However, hold 'em is also more counter-intuitive, which probably explains my observation. Anyway, some reasons why hold 'em players do poorly at stud are given below.

Reason No. 1: Hand values change more radically in stud. Two of the characteristics that make stud very different from hold 'em is that there are upcards and the starting hands are usually more sensitive to the number of players in the pot. This means that stud hands, in general, change value much more than hold 'em hands.

Here's an example. Suppose you start with:

Most hold 'em players will tell you that this is a very good hand. Of course they would be aware that it is not as good as a higher pair, but in general they want to play it. Experienced stud players know better. If their cards are dead, there are many situations

58

where they would simply fold even if it appears that it might be the best hand on third street.

Another example is a hand like a small pair with an ace kicker. Against one player it is definitely playable (assuming that your cards are live), but once several other players have come in, it loses much of it's value. This is because the probability of winning with two pair (and this includes aces-up) goes down faster than the size of the pot is going up. If several players stay until the river, you may discover that the two pair that you just made is simply a payoff hand, not a winning hand.

Reason No. 2: It is sometimes correct playing stud to take the third best hand and knock out the second best hand. This concept is very difficult for hold 'em players to feel comfortable with, but it is essential to winning stud play. The reason for this is that in stud it is very easy to improve to a hand that can frequently beat one opponent, but won't beat several.

Here's an example. Suppose on fifth street you have

The first player bets and you put him on pair of kings, and there are two players behind you. In most cases, your pair of fives is not the second best hand, but if you can get heads up against the probable kings and you improve to a small two pair, you stand a good chance of winning. Against three opponents, small two pair will almost never win. Thus, a raise is almost mandatory. (Also notice that this concept has some similarities to what we discussed in Reason No. 1, above.)

Reason No. 3: Reading hands is more difficult. Top hold 'em players are very adept at reading hands. In fact, this is one of the real separators of the experts from the merely good players. In stud, while reading hands is very important, it is also much harder to do accurately.

One reason for this is that your starting hand includes a third card and it is often difficult to figure out what it is. For instance, it may be fairly obvious that your opponent started with a pair of kings, but it may be very tough to figure out if he has made kings up or perhaps backed into a straight or a flush.

A second reason for this is that your hand or your opponents hand may go dead. An expert stud player may be able to conclude that in a certain situation, some particular hands have become unlikely for his opponent. This will allow him to make some strategy adjustments which may let him win an additional bet or even steal a pot. An example would be to bet an unimproved one pair on the river. The hold 'em regular won't make these plays himself, but will frequently be victimized by them.

This means that until you get a lot of experience playing stud, it is easy to get lost in the play of a hand. Hold 'em players who assume they are routinely reading well, will sometimes discover that they are trapped for extra bets because they didn't recognize where their opponent might be.

Reason No. 4: First round decisions are more crucial. There is no question that if you play the first round poorly at hold 'em you won't do very well. But it is also true that first round play at the hold 'em table is relatively easy. Thus, once a hold 'em player has a good grasp of opening round strategy, he should concentrate on playing the later streets. The best hold 'em players will (almost) all tell you that this is where the real money is made.

In many ways, stud is the opposite. Because you are starting with three cards instead of two, there are upcards to be accounted for, and the fact that stud hands are more sensitive to the number of players in the pot, third street in stud is much more important, and more difficult, than the first two cards in hold 'em. Typical hold 'em players tend to coast on the opening round in stud and consequently make mistakes they would never make at the hold 'em table.

Here's an example. Suppose you are dealt

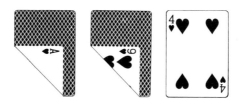

and your flush cards are live. Someone with a queen up raises in early position and you think that a likely hand for him is a pair of queens; you are on his immediate left. The typical hold 'em player will simply call, but the stud expert might not. He will consider how live his ace is (as well as his other cards) and will look around to see if any other queens are out. If conditions are favorable, he will now reraise in an attempt to play the pot heads-up. He may be able to win if he catches an ace, or makes two small pair. On the other hand, if his cards are dead he might fold.

Selecting the Best Game

In our book, *Gambling for a Living,* David Sklansky and I point out that even if you play well, game selection can be crucial to your long term success. This is particularly true if you play medium to high limits. When you enter a cardroom, consider putting your name on several different lists and be willing to change games once you start playing. You should try to get yourself in the game that is the most profitable and some criterions that you can use are described below.

Criterion No. 1: Look for a game with unknown faces. Most cardrooms have a core of regular players with whom the games are built around. Where I play, I am one of these regulars. Now some regulars play very well, and some don't. But in general, almost all regulars play better than the "tourists." Of course there are exceptions. There are a few regulars who play quite poorly, and sometimes an unknown player plays very well. But the vast majority of the time, if I don't know a player, their game can use a lot of improvement. So the first thing to look for is a game which features mostly unknown players.

Criterion No. 2: Look for a game that features a player who is guaranteed to lose all his money. Occasionally a player will show up who not only plays extremely poorly but who is guaranteed to lose all of his money once he starts losing. You should know this player based on prior experience, and this is a good reason why it is important to remember who you have previously played with.

Two words of caution. Sometimes these players will quit if they jump off a winner. Thus, it is important not to gamble with them when they first sit down. For example, if they want to put all of their money in when they are on a draw, and you are the favorite, don't do it!

Second, be aware that a drunk may appear to fit this criterion, but in my experience they usually don't. First, they can slow the game way down which can reduce your "earn." Second, and more importantly, after they lose a couple of hands they frequently get mad and quit. Thus, they don't lose all of their money, even though it appears they would.

Criterion No. 3: Look for a game that is passive and has medium size pots. Big pots do not necessarily mean good games. If the pots are large because of extremely aggressive play, this will put you in a situation where you can't play as many hands, and you will need to make some tough judgement decisions. What happens in this type of game is that unless you play extremely well, your win rate will drop, and your fluctuations will increase.

The best games, usually, are those that are moderately to very loose, but with little raising. This will allow you to play a few additional hands and, most important, it will allow you to manipulate your opponents in exactly the manner that you wish to. Weak players, whether weak-tight or just plain weak, are the most susceptible to manipulation. (Buying free cards, setting up bluffs, gaining overcalls, etc.)

Criterion No. 4: Staying away from games with top experts. Over the years I have learned that there is a difference between good players and great players. It's true that in poker if you play well, most of your profit comes from the bad players, but the top experts have a habit of getting in your way and disrupting your strategy. This can have the effect of steering the money away from you and towards them. Put another way, they have the ability to turn a pretty good player into a weak-tight player. At least they can do this in some situations. If you find yourself in a game with a player like this, I believe that you should try to sit as far away from him as possible. This way you will tangle with him less often. (Fortunately, unless you play very high, you won't run into too many players of this caliber. But be aware they do exist.)

Criterion No. 5: Look for players who don't automatically raise the blinds or bring-in if first in from late position. This is actually an extension of playing against weak opponents. Many players know that when they are first in from a late position they should automatically raise with most hands that they play. (There are actually a small number of exceptions, but they are beyond the scope of this essay.)[7] However, some weak players don't know this and you will see them frequently call when first in, late. This will allow you to pick up some pots that you would never normally win. In addition, it also allows you to better judge the strength of their hand. If they raise when first in, late, you know they are very strong. Against a good player who raises, you can never be this sure.

Criterion No. 6: Look for players who are known to select good games. This may seem a little trivial but it is something worth watching. There are a couple of players I know who are very conscious of selecting good games. Chances are, if you see one of them in a particular game, especially if it is not something they ordinarily play, there is a reason. Although this type of player probably plays well, it is often worth sitting down in a game simply because he has.

Criterion No. 7: Look for players who tip off what they are going to do. It's a significant advantage if you know what the players behind you are going to do. When playing poker, no matter what your game, you should always be looking to your left. Some players, particularly if they don't intend to play, will consistently be "announcing" what they intend to do. If you can see a couple of players folding out of turn, it is like being in late position even though you are not.

---

[7] See the "Loose Games" section in *Hold 'em Poker for Advanced Player: 21st Century Edition.*

Criterion No. 8: Look for games that are being played fast. This idea was alluded to above, and "being played fast" means that a lot of hands are dealt.

On a related note, there are a few players, especially at the hold 'em tables, who deliberately play very slowly in an attempt to discover what the action behind them will be like. While I agree that looking to your left has much value, there are a few players who carry this to such an extreme that they slow the game way down, and in many cases these games should be avoided. (I also don't believe that this "slow the game way down" is worth the effort. A quick look should gain you almost as much information as these annoying players get, and you won't irritate anyone.)

Finally, these ideas will do you the most good once you have learned to play reasonably well. If you play poorly and sit down in a good game you will only make it better. However, as stated in the introduction to this essay, if you play reasonably well, game selection is crucial to your overall success.

Visual Cues

One of the more controversial debates about poker is, "What are the value of tells?" In my opinion, they do have significant value, but only account for a small percentage of what an expert earns.

There are two reasons for this. First is reading hands. That is the "art and science" of deducing what cards your opponent holds. This is usually done by replaying the hand in your mind and combining it with whatever other information you have available about your opponent. If you can figure out your opponent's holding, you can now play perfectly.

The second reason is that in games like limit hold 'em and seven-card stud, the pots frequently get so large, in relation to the final bet, that you are often better off calling anyway. Using tells to fold when there are many chips in the center of the table can be a serious mistake. You may be costing yourself money even if you are only wrong occasionally.

This said, there is another area which is different from tells, but closely related, and I find fairly valuable. I call these visual cues.

The reason they are different is that they are not dependent on distinct mannerisms that players exhibit. In fact, as we shall soon see, they occur simply because many people are outright sloppy about their play, and you, the astute player, can take advantage of this sloppiness.

There are three spots where these visual cues are quite prevalent, and the rest of this essay will be devoted to describing them. Notice that they will allow you to play a few extra hands, steal a pot here and there, and occasionally gain an extra bet.

Visual Cue No. 1: Folding too soon before the flop. When playing hold 'em, many players quickly lose interest in their hands when they are not in blinds. This makes sense if you pick up something like

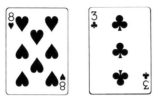

There is virtually no way you can play it, so the only thing you can do is toss it in the muck. So what happens is that many players begin their tossing motion before the action gets to them, and if you take quick look to your left, you can see this and take advantage of it.

For example, suppose you hold

in middle position and no one (except for the blinds) is in yet. Normally, this is a hand that I fold in this spot. But if three of the players behind me are beginning their pitching motions, my hand has become a late position steal and I'll put a in raise.

Before going on, it is important to note that only a quick look to your left is necessary. There are a few players who will take a long pause here and sometimes even hide their cards in an attempt to get the players to act behind them. This has the effect of slowing the game down too much and gains very little over what a quick look to your left can ascertain anyway.

Also, there are a few players who will indicate that they are going to play. While not as common, if you notice someone putting a chip on their cards or starting their betting motions you can profitably throw some hands away. For instance, if you are one off the button with the same Q♣T♥ as above, and you notice that the player on the button has put a chip on his cards, you might want to fold instead of raising.

It is also important to note that these comments do not apply to players who are in the blinds. In this spot, no matter how bad someone's hand is, they still have an interest in the pot. Thus they won't be sloppy anymore.

Finally, this visual cue mainly applies to hold 'em, since I virtually never see it in a stud game. This may have something to do with the fact that stud hands are more complex (because there are three cards instead of two and other upcards that supply information on the hand are available).

Visual Cue No. 2: Procrastinating stalls. Suppose you bet a very marginal hand on an early round. All your opponents fold except for one who takes a long time to call and is clearly having difficulty doing so. This is almost never an act, which means that you almost always have a profitable bluff on the next round. (Note that a profitable bluff doesn't mean that your opponent is guaranteed to fold. All it means is that given the size of the pot your opponent should fold often enough for you to make money in the long run.)

Here's an example from hold 'em. Suppose you have

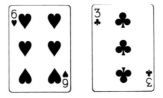

in the big blind, several players have limped in, and the flop is

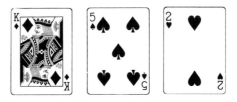

giving you a gutshot straight draw. Let's say you bet as a semi-bluff and everyone folds except for the player who is last to act, and he goes into one of these procrastinating stalls, indicating that he is not real happy about putting any more chips in the pot. You should bet again on fourth street no matter what hits unless it is a four that makes your straight — now you may want to check in an effort to trap your opponent.

Here's an example from stud. Suppose on third street you are first in from a late position and raise the bring-in with

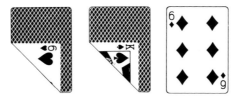

and the two remaining players behind you, each with a small card showing, call.

On fourth street it appears that everyone has caught a blank. You bet again and your first opponent tosses his hand, but your second opponent calls after a long pause, clearly struggling with his decision. You should bet again on fifth street unless you greatly improve your hand (where you now might want to check) or if your adversary now catches something that looks extremely threatening.

Visual Cue No. 3: Enough chips to call. The last visual cue we will examine is simply when your opponent prematurely grabs enough chips to call. This occurs when he expects you to bet, and he just wants to get the hand over with. In almost all cases he is just calling, because the pot is large and he can beat a bluff. At times I have even seen these callers put their money in the pot before their opponent has bet. How they now think that they can beat a bluff is something that I can't explain.

Anyway, the beauty of this is that since your opponent is almost always very weak, a marginal hand which you may or may not bet with now becomes a highly profitable bet. When you see this you should bet these hands every time. For example, when playing hold 'em, suppose you start with a pair of kings and the flop comes

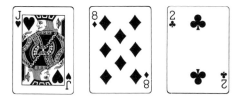

You bet and get one caller. The turn is the 9♥; you bet and your opponent calls again.

The river is a T♣. Notice that this card creates a problem for your hand because of the uniformity that it adds to the board. If you are not against a straight, you could easily be against two pair which beats your overpair. It's tough to bet in this spot.

But now suppose your opponent goes into one of these premature calls. You should bet virtually every time.

An example from stud would be when you have a medium strength hand, such as two pair and you are against someone who appears to be on a flush draw. Even though you have been betting all the way, your plan is to now check on the river. But to your surprise your opponent has enough chips in his hand and is ready to begin his calling motion. This almost always means that you are against something weak — your opponent either missed his flush and made a pair, or his hand was different from what you originally thought. In any case, you should bet almost every time.

What has happened, is that since you have led on every street, the player that you are against expects you to fire one more time, so his chips are ready to go in. Of course, thanks to his sloppy play he is right, your chips do go in and you almost always win an extra bet on the end.

To complete this "visual cue," it needs to be pointed out that the above is not a classic "acting tell." If your opponent was acting, he would almost always threaten you with enough chips to raise. If you saw this and your hand was weak, it might be more correct to bluff with a terrible hand, than value bet a marginal one.

To conclude this essay, I stress again, these visual cues occur due to sloppy play. It is very rare for a strong player to play sloppily. Top players pay attention to what they are doing and what is going on. If you see something similar to what is described above and it comes from an expert or near expert player, there may be a reason, and you should proceed with caution.

Some Quick Thoughts

Here are a few quick thoughts which some of you may find helpful.

The best starting hand in seven-card stud is three aces and the best starting hand in hold 'em is of course two aces. But there is a big difference between the strength of these hands. The reason is that it is much more difficult to have three aces beat than it is to have two of them snapped off. Thus, if you are first in with three aces in a stud game, you should virtually never raise. Winning only the antes is a disaster for this hand, and having the ace up will tend to scare off your opponents.

In hold 'em, the opposite is true. Since you have no card exposed, you don't have an upcard to slow your opponents down. Furthermore, even though you would prefer to do better than just win the blinds, it is not the disaster it is in stud, since, as we all know, a pair of aces in a hold 'em game is no cinch.

♣ ♦ ♥ ♠

Most tournaments are essentially no-limit contests, or if you think this is too extreme, they at least have a no-limit aspect to them. This is simply because once you get past the early stages of a tournament, many hands are played where one of the contestants will be all in before the river. There will also be more one-on-one confrontations due to the tendency for many players to tighten up in tournaments, again, mimicking a no-limit game.

This should have many implications concerning your proper strategy. One of them is that hands such as high pairs in stud and ace-big card in hold 'em, go up in value because they frequently win without improving. (Notice that this is similar to how you would want to play if you were all in.)

72

On the other hand, holdings like a small three flush in a stud game or a suited-connector in hold 'em lose value, for when they do mature to a pat hand, even though you win the pot, there may not be anyone left to collect additional bets from.

By the way, this may also partially explain why some people who have terrific tournament records seem to give their money away in the side games, and why some of the best side game players perform poorly in tournaments. It may also help explain why there are very few side game players who are good at more than one form of poker, but why many of the best tournament players do well, regardless of the type of poker that the tournament is based on.

♣ ♦ ♥ ♠

There are many spots in tournaments where you must play your hand differently from the way you would want to play if in a side game. One time is when you are a big favorite to win the hand but would be a slightly smaller favorite, if you were to play it the side game way. The reason for this is that even though you might have a huge advantage, losing the hand that small percentage of the time is something that you might not be able to afford to do in a tournament. In a side game, you may not like it, but you will eventually recover from the loss.

The opposite is also sometimes true early in a tournament. Here you might be willing to take a little the worst of it, knowing that if you get lucky and win the pot, it will give you a lot of chips to work with. An example is calling before the flop with a small pair in hold 'em where it is fairly clear that you won't get the required implied odds to make this call profitable. In a side game you would throw your hand away. But in a tournament, you may want to go ahead and play, since gaining chips will allow you to attack the small stacks later on. (Actually this is theoretically in error. However, it does increase your hourly rate since your expectation remains about the same, but your average time played goes down.)

♣ ♦ ♥ ♠

The number one error that many relatively new players make when playing poker is that they do not take into account the size of the pot. Typically they will reason out that their chances of having the best hand is not very good, so they throw their hand away. This can be referred to as the "Fit or Fold Concept." The problem with this, is that when the pot gets large you often don't need that good of a hand to make the call. This might be because you only need a small chance to improve for your call to be profitable, or on the end, you only need a small chance for your opponent to be betting a weaker hand than yours for your call to be correct.

On the other hand, there are situations that occasionally develop where you can be absolutely sure that you are beat, and thus, can throw away a reasonable hand even with a large pot. These usually occur against a player who virtually never bluffs or would never bluff in this particular situation. They can also sometimes be determined by good card reading skills.

An example would be when you have a relatively strong hand and have played it that way, but you get raised on the end by a timid player. Since he should expect you to call, (it is fairly obvious that you have a good hand), you might want to throw away some of the lesser hands that you would normally bet with in this spot, (and perhaps only call with some hands that you might reraise a more aggressive player with).

♣ ♦ ♥ ♠

Your required bankroll is predicated on two parameters. The first is your expectation, also known as your win rate, and the second is your level of fluctuations which can be measured by the (statistical) standard deviation. (Yes, you can measure luck.) What's interesting is that in this relationship, the higher your win rate, the smaller the bankroll that you need, while the higher your standard deviation, the higher the bankroll that you need.

However, it is very unlikely to move one of these parameters up or down without affecting the other.

Let's look at two simple cases. Suppose you are a strong winning player and decide to double your stakes. How does this affect your bankroll? First, since the players tend to get tougher as you move up in limit, your win rate, while it may go higher, will not usually double. Second, since the players are tougher, and frequently more aggressive, your standard deviation could more than double. This means that if you double your limit, you may easily need three to four times as much money to assure survival. Of course this all depends on the particular player and the particular game that he is moving to. But when you make a significant move up, be prepared for a bumpy ride.

The second case is what happens when the game goes short handed. Assuming that you play this form of poker well and that you are in a good spot, your win rate will certainly increase. But you will now be in a situation where you are playing many more hands than what you normally would in a ring game, and many of these hands will only have marginal value at best. Here again, your standard deviation can increase dramatically. Thus, you may easily need a larger bankroll to assure survival if you frequently find yourself in this spot.

♣ ♦ ♥ ♠

Once you get past the lower limits in stud, and this usually means you reach $15-$30 or higher, the ante becomes a significant influence on correct strategy (because it is proportionally higher). This frequently means that hands, that at first look like drawing hands, are in reality better off being played heads-up. For example, in many spots you would much rather play a small or medium pair with a large overcard kicker against only one player, even if he probably holds a big pair.

There are several reasons for this. First, you may not be against the hand your opponent is representing. Second, you can frequently win if you now make two little pair. And third, the ante does make a difference.

♣ ♦ ♥ ♠

In a standard no-limit ring game, when someone bets a stack of chips on the flop, they are frequently saying that they are prepared to follow it up with a bet of several stacks on the next round. This has a major impact on strategy. However, in a no-limit *tournament*, this aspect of standard no-limit play diminishes because in many instances at least one of the players will run out of chips. Thus, the bettor does not have to worry about facing this situation. Not only does this mean that some of the skill of no limit play is removed from the tournaments, but it also means that you can be much more daring with your bets in a tournament than you would at a full table in a side game where all the players had an adequate number of chips in front of them. (Again notice that this may help explain why some tournament experts seem to perform poorly in side games. Not having to play the last couple of rounds makes tournament play a "weak" form of no limit.)

♣ ♦ ♥ ♠

Again, one of the most common errors that beginning to intermediate players make, is that they don't take into account the size of the pot.) For instance, on our forum at www.twoplustwo.com, we frequently see questions where someone asks if a fold they made with a relatively good hand was correct. The problem with their questions is that we are not told enough about the betting action to know how big the pot is. Just because it is likely that you have the second best hand, does not mean that a fold is correct. In large pots, your hand only has to be good every now and then for you to commit those final chips into the pot.)

This idea also should affect calling strategy on the earlier streets as well. There are many spots where it might be clear that you hold a second- or third-best hand yet the size of the pot indicates a call.

♣ ♦ ♥ ♠

It hard to believe, but someone who never bluffs is frequently playing as badly as someone who bluffs half the time (when he misses his hand). This is easy to see as follows. Suppose on the end your opponent bets. If it is someone who never bluffs, your expectation for that bet is simply zero, since you never call. If it is someone who bluffs half the time, you now call every time (because of the size of the pot) and again your expectation for that bet is zero since you win his bet half the time and lose your bet half the time. Notice that in both cases you always win the pot when you are entitled to it. (To simplify things I'm neglecting those time when you both have good hands. However, in the long run these should roughly break even and there should be little impact on your overall results.)

♣ ♦ ♥ ♠

To be successful in tough games, which usually means $30-$60 or higher, it's important that you not be too consistent in your betting strategy. One spot, where even most good players fall down, is on the end. For example, there are almost no hold 'em players who, if they bet the flop, and bet the turn, will then try to check raise the river. Part of the reason for this is that against weaker players it doesn't really hurt if you bet the river after betting on the previous rounds (when a non-threatening card hits) since this type of player will not usually bet for value with a hand of only moderate strength, even if you check. However, against the better players you are giving up too much information. Not only will some of them be willing to bet weaker hands for value, but they will bluff at an appropriate frequency as well. Against this type of player, you must occasionally try to get two bets on the end. Not only will you sometimes make extra money, in the future, when you do check a weaker hand, they should be more inclined to check it down themselves.

♣ ♦ ♥ ♠

I have always been critical of those individuals who do "hot and cold" computer simulations and then try to derive proper hold 'em strategy based on these results. However, these results can be very valuable in the hands of an experienced hold 'em player. That is because expert players will know what adjustments need to be made.

More recently, computer programs have been produced that now play hold 'em with a moderately sophisticated strategy. Unfortunately, they don't play as well as an expert, (and probably couldn't beat most $10-$20 games), but their results are certainly better than "hot and cold" simulations. But are they really?

Since these programs still need improvement in their play, their results will also need adjustment, but now the expert can't do it. The reason is that since he doesn't know exactly what the programming code says, he won't know exactly what adjustments need to be made. Thus, even though their results are much better than "hot and cold" simulations, conclusions made from these results can be much more dangerous than conclusions made from automatically playing all hands to the river.

♣ ♦ ♥ ♠

In hold 'em, once you have mastered a reasonably good starting hand strategy, it doesn't help much if you improve it. The real money is made by playing well from the flop on. But the opposite is not true. If you choose a terrible starting hand strategy, you should lose all your money no matter how well you play from the flop on. For instance, if you decide to call many raises with hands that have the potential to trap you for many bets, expect to lose all your money no matter how well you play on the later streets. It's true you might lose it a little slower than someone who also plays badly on the later streets, but you will still lose it all.

♣ ♦ ♥ ♠

It's been my experience that against weak players, short handed stud is much more profitable than short-handed hold 'em. The reason for this is that giving free cards is much more damaging to the weak stud player than it is to the weak hold 'em player. This has something to do with the fact that in stud each player has his own board to work with instead of sharing a community board with the other players. Put another way, in stud, the player with the stronger board is often going to win the pot on his board strength alone. If you fail to take advantage of this fact, many hands which you should automatically win can go to your opponent.

As an obvious example, suppose on fifth street you have a three flush showing. This should be an automatic bet, and if your opponent has a weak hand, which will often be the case in a short-handed pot, he will fold. But if you choose to check it down, you will give away a large percentage of these pots.

♣ ♦ ♥ ♠

Most beginning players feel that hold 'em is a more difficult game to master than seven-card stud. This has a lot to do with the fact that many hold 'em concepts seems counter-intuitive, while stud plays in a more straight forward fashion. In reality, I believe the opposite is true. I do agree that many hold 'em concepts are in fact very counter-intuitive, and because of this, hold 'em games should stay good for a very long time. But in stud, you have to take into account the effect of upcards and also consider the fact that stud hands are more sensitive to the number of players in the pot. This means that arriving (in your mind) at the correct value of a stud hand is more difficult than understanding the worth of a hold 'em hand. Thus, stud is a little harder to play at an expert level. However, neither game is easy; and only a relatively small number of players can claim to be expert at either of them.

♣ ♦ ♥ ♠

There are many different figures floating around as to how much the best poker players make. When I'm asked, I usually say a little better than one big bet per hour. This is based on my personal experience after playing for many years. But I'm also referring to middle limit games. At the higher limits the players get tougher and the win rates of the very best players usually drop. It is a rare high limit player who does better than two-thirds of a big bet per hour (in the long run), and most are happy with making a little better than half a big bet an hour.

Ironically, the most successful high limit players are not the ones who are the best at some particular game. They are the ones who can play several games well.

General Concepts

Afterthought

I believe that the most important essay in this section is "Playing for Minimum Wage." This is because poker is fairly easy to beat. That's right, you just read it, "Poker is fairly easy to beat." In fact, if you have some sense and do a little bit of work, you should have no trouble winning. Just learn to play tight; play in small games against many players who possess virtually no skill, and you should have no trouble overcoming the rake.

But there is a problem. You won't overcome the rake by much; and in my opinion poker really won't be worth it for most of you. It might be a little fun, but it won't be very rewarding; and if you could do much better at it you will probably discover that poker is a lot of fun as well as very rewarding.

Of course, to do well at poker requires much skill that can sometimes take years to develop. We saw this in the "Struggling to be Good" essay and this idea appears in many other spots as well, especially in "Five Skills to Work On."

When at the tables, I'm always sitting in games where the long term reward for the highly skilled player is worthwhile — specifically at least $30 per hour and sometimes much higher. This can vary depending on the limit, exactly how well you play, and the quality of the game. But I strongly feel that $30 is the minimum for an expert, and many do much better than that.

Part Two
Technical Ideas

Technical Ideas

Introduction

When I began to play poker seriously I thought the game would be a "snap" because of my mathematical background. Even if there were other aspects of poker such as psychology, because of the math I would still have a big jump on the competition. Was I in for a surprise.

On the other hand, there definitely is a technical side to poker. It may not be quite as important as I originally thought, but it does have a fair amount of value, and understanding these ideas will help your overall performance at the poker tables. So don't neglect it.

Which is Bigger?

One question that I hear poker players debate is which game is bigger, seven-card stud or Texas hold 'em? The stud advocates will tell you that there are five betting rounds instead of four, that it is much easier to draw out so that there is much more chasing, and that calling a bet on sixth street is usually automatic. The hold 'em advocates will tell you that there are more mutiway pots, the betting on the first round is often two full bets as opposed to a bring-in, and the large luck factor that is present between the first two cards and the flop encourages maniacal play. So who is right?

During the past few years, I and an associate have been collecting data on both games, and we have come to some surprising conclusions. My friend is an expert stud player and a very good hold 'em player. We have kept careful track of our results and now have good estimates of "our" standard deviations for some of the games that are spread in Las Vegas. At first we found these results to be somewhat contradictory, but I now believe that we understand exactly what they mean. Also, you need to understand that everyone plays differently, and games in different locations can have different levels of fluctuations. So our conclusions may not be true in all situations, but I believe in general, they are fairly accurate.

(For those of you not familiar with the "standard deviation," let's just say that it is a measure of how much short term luck there is in a poker game, and short term luck determines how big a poker game is. That is, the bigger the standard deviation, the bigger the game.)

To start, lets look at something obvious. If you were in Las Vegas and went to The Mirage and compared the $20-$40 stud game to the $20-$40 hold 'em game you would notice the hold 'em game has far more chips on the table, per person, than the stud game. And the pots, usually, are much larger. A typical hold 'em game generally has many more mutiway pots than the stud game. And, a typical hold 'em hand has many more raises than the typical stud hand. Thus, it seems obvious that hold 'em should produce a much higher standard deviation than stud, and therefore be considered the bigger game. But our results show an hourly standard deviation of $280 for the $20-$40 hold 'em and $350 for the $20-$40 stud. This brings us to the surprising conclusion that if your skills are somewhere between that of a "live one" to a marginal player, then hold 'em is bigger. If your skills are somewhere between playing pretty good to expert, then stud is the bigger game. (We also have results, again based on our play, for higher limit games which are consistent with these numbers, but for purposes of this essay I will not address them at this time.)

(For some of you who also track your standard deviation, these results may appear small. What we have discovered is that as the years have gone by our standard deviations have dropped. We suspect that this may have something to do with our hand reading skills improving.)

So why is this the case? Why does the expert hold 'em player have more control over his results than the expert stud player, while the live one will swing more wildly in hold'em than he does at stud.

We believe it is the result of two reasons. First, reading hands may be more effective in hold 'em. You only have to figure out two cards instead of three, and you get to see your opponent's last card. This impacts your results in two ways. When playing stud, you may know your opponent's primary hand, such as two aces, but you won't know his kicker; or you may know he started with a three flush, but will have no idea if he improves his hand in other ways. On the end, when playing stud, you frequently have to call because of the size of the pot. In hold 'em, even though the pot may be bigger than it is in stud, you can sometimes safely throw your hand away. If the flush card gets there, you may know without question (if you are an expert card reader) that you are beat.

The other reason is that the expert stud player plays looser than the expert hold 'em player. In fact, as your stud game improves, you will gradually find yourself playing more hands, while the opposite is frequently true for hold 'em players. There are many reasons for this, but two of them are that in stud you can adjust hand values based on the upcards, and you can often call for just the bring-in bet. Hold 'em seems to work just the opposite. The better you play, the more traps you try to avoid, thus many players concede that their hold 'em games tighten up as their skills get better.

This brings us to a final and somewhat entertaining conclusion. If you are talking to another poker player and he begins to argue that hold 'em is the bigger game, then it may be safe to assume that he "plays poorly." On the other hand, if he argues that stud is bigger, not only might this be an expert player, but you probably won't want to play in *any* game with him, whether it be stud or hold 'em.

A Note on Bluffing

Players often ask how often should you bluff? People new to poker commonly think this is the main part of the game. But many participants who have played for a long time virtually never bluff. They consider it a "sucker play." Let's see who's right.

To answer this question, let's begin by analyzing a simple question regarding bluffing. Suppose there are two players, lets call them A and B. They play exactly the same, except that on the end Player A will bluff 50 percent of the time and Player B will never bluff. Who do you think plays worse? (Before you go on, stop and think, and also try to come up with a reason to go along with your answer.) We will assume they are playing either a typical limit hold 'em game or a typical limit stud game.

Well, if your answer was Player A you are wrong, and if your answer was Player B you are also wrong. It turns out that both A and B play equally bad. (For your information my experience is that most people answer Player A, the person who bluffs half the time.)

To see why this is so, lets see what happens if you are against Player A. Since he bluffs half the time you should call him every time. Thus, half the time you will lose an additional bet, but this will be canceled out by the other half of the time when you win an additional bet. Your expectation on the end will be zero. That is, in the long run Player A will neither gain nor lose bets against you.

Now let's see what happens against Player B. Since he never bluffs, you should never call. Your expectation on the end is also zero because you never give up a bet that you shouldn't. So again Player B, like Player A, will neither gain nor lose bets against you.

(I'm aware that you may occasionally hold a strong hand that you will play — perhaps with a raise — no matter who bets. But for practical purposes, these hands have no impact on the result of this question.)

This brings us to an interesting conclusion: Someone who never bluffs plays as badly as someone who bluffs half the time. This is also why most people pick Player A. They recognize that someone who bluffs half the time plays terribly, but they equate someone who never bluffs as being a tight player, and they perceive playing tight as playing reasonably well. But in this situation, this is clearly not the case.

Now we come to a related question. If never bluffing is terrible, and bluffing half the time is terrible, how often should you bluff? Some of you will quickly say 25 percent, or one-fourth of the time, since this is the mid-point between the two extremes with no expectation. But this answer is also wrong.

Without going into the mathematics of bluffing, it turns out that the proper bluffing frequency is usually dependent on the size of the bet relative to the size of the pot. The larger the bet in relation to the pot, the more you should bluff, and the smaller the bet in relation to the pot, the less you should bluff.

The reason I say usually, and not always, is that your opponent can radically change your bluffing frequency. Against someone who almost always calls, you might never bluff, and against someone who doesn't call nearly enough, you might want to bluff more. However, in many situations the above guideline is right on the money.

Suppose you are in your typical game, either limit hold 'em or seven-card stud. The pot is fairly large and all the cards are out. Yes, you should bluff, but only occasionally.

I recently saw some similar advice which stated that in most popular forms of poker spread in our public cardrooms you should do very little bluffing. I agree with this advice, especially late in the hand. (Early in the hand this is not true. There are many situations where it is correct to semi-bluff. But that is a different subject.)

However, there is a difference between not bluffing much and not bluffing at all. Many people who are trying to play well recognize that it is not correct to do much bluffing on the end in limit games, so they quit bluffing altogether. But when they do this, they are now playing as badly as Player B (who plays as badly as Player A).[8]

This brings us to our final conclusion. Bluffing is an important part of poker, and to be a successful player you should be prepared to do your share. It's true that many poor players bluff too much, and this costs them plenty. But if you think the solution for this is to never bluff, you will also be costing yourself much more than you would like to think about.

---

[8] To be honest this statement is not completely true when playing against real opponents. The reason of course is that many players will sometimes pay off a non-bluffer on the end hoping that this time will somehow be an exception. Thus someone who never bluffs will do a bit better than the chronic bluffer.

Looking at the Flop

When striving to become an expert player, you must take into account the size of the pot. Most players don't do a good job in this area. They are vaguely aware that in larger pots you should call more and slowplay less, and they will often put in an extra bet or raise in an effort to gain a free card or to knock someone out. But what they rarely account for is how the cards and the pot size can affect your opponent's hand.

Let me give a moderately complex example. It was a hand that I played in a $40-$80 hold 'em game a couple of years ago at The Mirage. It was an unraised six-way pot where I had limped in early with a pair of nines. The flop came

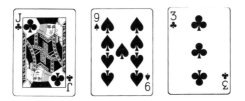

The player in the small blind checked, the player in the big blind, who was on my immediate right, bet, and there were three players still to act behind me. I was next, and I had the choice to either call or raise.

Many of you will say that raising is the proper play, and several of the newer hold 'em books advise to play your hand fast in this spot. They argue that you should lower the odds for drawing hands, but I disagree. The reason for this is that you will not be able to knock out anyone who has a quality draw like two clubs (giving him a four-flush), or queen-ten or ten-eight (which gives him an open end straight draw). Against these hands I prefer to see what comes on fourth street. If a dangerous card hits I'll be happy I didn't raise. If a blank comes I might be able to extract two double size bets from the drawing hands when they are more than a 4-to-1 dog. Putting this in more technical terms I am playing my hand in such a way that I am reducing their "effective" odds, not their current pot odds. (See *The Theory of Poker* by David Sklansky for more discussion on effective odds.)

Deviating slightly, it is important to realize that if a blank hits on the turn my opponents are bigger dogs than it will appear to them. The reason for this is that a flush card could come on the river that will also pair the board. (Of course if the straight card now comes, the board cannot pair, since a blank hit on fourth street.)

However, if that "blank" on the turn is another trey, all of these draws will now be "drawing dead." The same is true if either a jack or a nine comes.

Returning to our example, if I raise, hands like middle pair and gut shot draws will probably be folded. Given that I had flopped middle set, it is to my benefit to have these hands to stay in. The person with a pair is drawing almost dead against my hand, and the player with a gut shot now needs about 14-to-1 for his call to be correct, and if I only call he will be getting 8-to-1 (assuming no one else plays). (As already mentioned, with two cards to come I can fill up even if he makes his hand. Thus his true odds are higher than the chances that he will make his hand.)

Consequently, I called; two of the players called behind me; the player in the small blind position then raised (to my surprise), and the player between us called. Many of you will say that it's now the same situation again, but it is actually very different. If I call there will now be fourteen bets in the pot, and it will be correct for anyone with a gut shot to call, and I don't want them to make this play correctly. Consequently, a raise is now the right play.

This hand represents an important idea that is present in all of poker. Once a pot gets large, you usually need to follow a strategy that maximizes your chance of winning it. You also need to be conscious of the cards that are present and the possible hands that are out. Many players are aware of the first idea. They understand that you want to win as many big pots as possible and that making them a little bigger is frequently the wrong way to go. But what they are not aware of is how the cards that are present can impact your decisions.

For instance, if the flop above did not contain two suited cards or two cards close together in rank, I would not have raised on the flop the second time around. It would have been proper to wait for the turn to become aggressive.

The key to playing this hand correctly is to understand where your maximum profit comes from. It does not come from raising on the flop, and it does not come from slowplaying your set in an effort to "suck others in." It comes from the combination of being able to save money when the future cards come scary, and gaining money when the future cards are either blanks or pair the board. The maximum profit also comes from understanding what the cards on board mean in relation to the size of the pot and your particular hand. To become an expert player, you must be able to look at the flop and very quickly know what it represents and how it can impact the hand that you are holding.

It Doesn't Matter

Recently, an acquaintance in the poker room wanted my opinion on limping with aces one off the button in a limit hold 'em game. Apparently, another writer had recommended this play in his poker column. (By the way, I'm not sure which writer it was or how truly enthusiastic he was about this play.) My answer was that it probably didn't matter and that surely there were many more important things to be concerned with when sitting at the hold 'em table.

But my friend persisted, so we went through a quick analysis which I'm going to repeat here. First, notice that it is 220-to-1 to be dealt a pair of aces. This means that if you are in a game that deals 35 hands per hour — which is typical for many games — you should see aces approximately once for every six hours that you play. Sometimes you'll get them more often, but sometimes it will be much longer than six hours between aces. But on average, once every six hours is roughly correct.

In a ten-handed game, even though you will be getting aces once every six hours, you will only be in any particular position one-tenth of the time. Thus you can expect to have aces one off the button approximately once in every 60 hours.

The next question is, how often, when you are dealt aces one off the button, will everyone pass to you? Now there is no simple formula. In a tight game everyone will pass more often than in a loose game, and in some "no-fold 'em" games this situation will virtually never occur. But in the games I play, my best guess, and this is based on my judgment and experience, is that everyone will fold to the player one off the button a little less than one-fourth of the time. Thus the opportunity to make this play should occur approximately once every 250 hours.

To put this in perspective, if you were to play hold 'em 20 hours a week, 50 weeks a year, the opportunity to limp in first, one off the button, with a pair of aces would happen just four times in that year. So we already see that it doesn't happen very often.

The next question is, when it happens, how close is it whether you raise or just call. Again I must answer using my judgment. My best guess is that it is fairly close. That is, the difference between your results when you have a pair of aces one off the button, no one else is in, and you raise or call, won't be much.

Of course there could be an occasional exception, depending on who is in the blind and how that person perceives you. But in general you are looking at a very close play that rarely happens. *Conclusion: Think about something more worthwhile.*

Now the reason I bring this up is that this is an area where a lot of aspiring players get bogged down. In an effort to play better they direct their efforts on starting hand strategy and neglect play from the flop on. What they fail to realize is that once you have mastered starting hand strategy reasonably well, you only gain pennies by improving on it and may be costing yourself many dollars if you neglect the rest of your game.

On our forum, at www.twoplustwo.com, we see these types of questions all the time. For example, there has been much debate over whether ace-nine suited is a better hand than king-queen offsuit, and whether it is ever correct to play five-four offsuit on the button if several people have just limped in. The fact is that the absolutely correct answers to these questions are unimportant to your long-term success.

I do need to point out that proper strategy on your first two cards is very important. For example, it you routinely call raises with hands like

that can easily make second best hands and can cause you to lose many bets, your overall performance should be poor at the hold 'em tables.

So what's the final conclusion? If you are new to hold 'em, you need to make sure that you learn how to play your first two cards well. If you are an experienced player and you have poor results, it is probably worth your time to review play of your starting hands. However, if you know that your starting hand strategy is reasonably good, then your time is much better spent on improving your play from the flop on than it is by trying to find some small edge that you might be missing during the first round.

It is my experience that no matter how well you play on the later streets there is always room for improvement, and this improvement can sometimes contribute quite significantly to your overall results. The true experts excel on all rounds. If you are hoping to achieve this status, you must be able to do the same.

Searching for the Right Limit

Let's start with a little history. A few years ago there was a $75-$150 seven-card stud game that went every day at The Mirage in Las Vegas, and on some days there would be several such games. In other words, the game was very successful and clearly stood the test of time.

Now when I say successful I'm talking about a game that produces a proper balance of luck and skill for those players who participate in it. This means that there is enough luck so that weak players will have some winning nights, but enough skill is also available so that the better players will do well in the long run, and thus, form a core around which the game can be built.

But there was a problem. There was also a very successful $20-$40 limit game, but nothing in between. To solve this problem it was decided by top cardroom management to start a $40-$80 game (with a $10 ante). In my opinion, this was a terrible mistake.

Again a little history. Many years ago, The Mirage management decided not to spread a $50-$100 (with a $10 ante). My understanding was that it was felt that this limit was too close in size to the $75-$150, and it might cannibalize this highly successful game. I believe that this would have happened, so this decision made sense to me.

Anyway, after a few changes in leadership, the new Mirage poker room management decided to go with the game in the middle. Even though their intentions were good, they didn't realize that it is not necessarily the betting limits that determine the "size" of a game, but its starting structure. With a $10 ante you should play more hands when the bets are in $40 increments as opposed to $50. This means you should limp in more, call more raises (and raise more yourself), and call more reraises. Thus the $40-$80 game with the $10 ante is essentially the same size game as a $50-$100 game with a $10 ante. It wasn't long before this game began to impact the $75-$150.

In stud, it is possible to achieve tremendous skill. More so than in hold 'em. This has a lot to do with the fact that unlike hold 'em, there are upcards, and that stud hands are more sensitive to the number of players in the pot. This means that unless something is done, the balance of luck and skill at these higher limits, where these great players reside, has the potential to lose balance.[9]

But stud has something that hold 'em doesn't have: Antes. And, by adjusting these antes, the better players can be handicapped so that the balance of luck and skill remains intact. That's why the $75-$150 game has evolved to a $15 ante over many years. This would be like playing $15-$30 with a $3 ante instead of the current $2 ante. In other words, this increase in ante relative to the bet size has the effect of handicapping the great players (who graduated from the $15-$30 games long ago), so that their advantage over "live ones" is not too great.

(The larger relative ante will also increase your short term fluctuations. But that is another subject that will not be discussed here.)

However, the $40-$80 game played with a $10 ante (as well as the $80-$160 game played with a $20 ante) went too far in my opinion. It handicapped the better players too much, and upset the balance of luck and skill that poker games require to thrive. The result has been a decrease in high limit stud in Las Vegas. While hold 'em continues to thrive, stud above the $20-$40 limit has not done well recently. The $40-$80 struggles to continue on a regular basis. Too many good players are competing against one another at the $30-$60 limit (with a $5 ante), and the $80-$160 game is not as strong as the $75-$150 game used to be. Something must be altered.

---

[9] I want to note that only a small number of players have been able to become this skillful. But they do exist.

(Note: If stud was played five handcd, the $40-$80 structure that I am criticizing might be okay. But since most games are played eight handed, this is not the case.)

So what needs to change? It must be realized that these structures have evolved over time; they did not appear by accident. This means that when cardroom management makes what appears to be small changes in their games, they should often think twice and ask the question whether this change has the potential to upset the balance of luck and skill that is so essential in keeping poker rooms thriving.

Comparing the Rake

As the majority of you know, I live in Las Vegas and this is where most of my poker is played. It means that I pay one of the lowest rakes in the country. Specifically, the game that I have been playing most recently is $30-$60 hold 'em. At The Bellagio, I pay $5 per half hour to play this game. If I were to play the same game in California, I would be paying almost as much as twice this rate depending on the location. So this brings forth the obvious question. Is the rake in California too high, or is Las Vegas ridiculously cheap?

To address this question, let's look at a different poker topic that we are all familiar with — bluffing. Top poker players know that if you bluff too much, you are not playing very well, and if you bluff too little you are not playing very well. That is there should be an optimal bluffing frequency that assures you maintain a certain level of profits. The same should hold for the rake.

If I ran a cardroom, my goal would be to set the rake at that level which maximizes my profits over the long haul. Obviously if I didn't charge poker players to play, or charged very little the cardroom would lose money and eventually go out of business. On the other hand, if I charged way too much, everyone would be losers; the games would cease to exist, and again the cardroom would go out of business.

Notice, then, there should be an optimal amount to charge. This amount would allow the house to make a reasonable profit, but would also keep the games thriving. That is, a core of regular players would develop to start games and keep the games going; and poker as an industry would grow.

What's interesting about this is that most players will tell you that the rake in California is ridiculous. They say, "Compared to Vegas it is way too high." I disagree. In fact, in my opinion the rake in California is much lower than it is in Las Vegas. At least if I lived in a place like Los Angeles or San Jose, that would be the case *for me*. Perhaps not with you, but if I lived in one of these locations, the clubs would be paying me to play. That is my rake would be reversed.

Many California Cardrooms are built on what is known as the prop system. This includes "silent," as well as "regular" props. For those of you who don't know, a silent prop is a player who is paid by the house to play in a particular game. He puts his name on the list like a regular player, and like a regular player he can't be pulled from the game. (He also usually doesn't get paid as much as a "regular" prop, but the salary can still be pretty good. I should know. Many years ago, when the Bicycle Club first opened, I worked [for about three months] as a silent prop in their $25-$50 draw games on the weekends.)

So what does this mean in relation to the rake? It means that the true rake the house collects is not as high as it seems. Even though a game might be full, if a couple of props are sitting at the table, the California cardroom is collecting less for itself than the cardrooms in Las Vegas, even though Nevada cardrooms generally have a lower rake. In other words, the rake in California is not very fair. Some people are paying "double rake," while others aren't paying any rake at all.

But why do props even exist? The California cardrooms will tell you that they are needed to start games and keep games going. They are needed because there are not enough regular players. This is clearly the case because when the regular player population base gets large enough, most California Cardrooms do eliminate some of their prop jobs.

This leads to an interesting conclusion. If the rake was lower, this extra money which the players would "hold," would do exactly what the prop salary does. That is, it would create more regular players who would start games and keep the games going and there would be no need for props

However, it gets even better than this. I believe that the more poker players there are, the more poker players there will be. We players tell our friends what a great game this is and recruit new people to the cardrooms all the time. In addition, a lower rake will allow more players to get through that initial survival period, again producing more long term customers for the cardrooms.

So the final conclusion is this: In the long run, a fair and equitable rake will be better for players, and better for those cardrooms that adopt it. It may lower a cardroom's profits today, but it will greatly enhance them and allow our industry to grow at an optimal rate in the future.

Detrimental is Good

Even though I am known, primarily, as a hold 'em player, I have played a great deal of seven-card stud. There are several reasons for this, but most importantly is that I believe more money can be made there. (Of course, this depends on the particular game. If several live ones are sitting at a hold 'em table, and the stud game is full of regulars, then hold 'em will obviously be the best choice. But if both lineups look about the same, I believe the stud expert has a higher expectation.)

So why can the expert win more playing stud than hold 'em? There are many reasons. This essay will discuss three of them. Two are strategic and one has to do with the structure of the game itself.

The two strategic reasons:
1. Upcards are available, and
2. Stud hands are more sensitive to whether they are being played short handed or multiway.

What this means is that hands in stud vary more in value than hands in hold 'em, and the typical player does not do a good job adjusting for hand strength. In many situations they put in too much money on pairs, and don't do as good a job as they should knocking people out.

However, my purpose in writing this essay is not to go into strategic detail. I want to discuss another idea which is very important to long term profit potential in poker. It is the idea that stud structure usually changes as you move up in limit, while hold 'em structure does not.

First, I need to point out that this idea only comes into play if you either participate in the bigger games or have aspirations of doing so, and when I say bigger games, I'm referring to $40-$80 or higher. Second, and this statement will appear very ironic, the change in stud structure as you move up in limit, will be detrimental to the good players which is precisely the reason it allows them to win more.

To see why this is true, let's look at high limit hold 'em. One of the things that happens in all poker, is that as you move up in limits, the games are generally tougher. (The reason I say generally is that there are always exceptions and you should be on the look out for these.) This almost always translates into tighter games, and if poker games become tight enough, they will cease to exist. Those bad players who crave action, won't get enough, and those good players who take advantage of bad players won't have the bad players available to them. This is precisely what happens in high limit hold 'em, and is why you do not see many high limit hold 'em games.

The same phenomenon also occurs in stud. The better players move up, and these are, in general, the players who play a little tighter. But just playing tight at high limit stud won't make it. The reason for this is that in stud, unlike hold 'em, there is a progressive ante. Generally, the higher you play, the larger the ante is, in proportion to the bet. This requires play that is a little looser, but more importantly, it handicaps the best players by reducing their advantage on third street and forces them to play the other streets very well in order to gain back their edge.

Getting back to high limit hold 'em, since there is no structure change, the best players are not handicapped by the structure. Now when a weak player sits down, he won't have a chance. He will usually lose his money quickly and will want to find another game. And when he wins, his wins will generally be small since he won't be getting the action that he thinks he deserves. Hence, the advantage these top players have is just too great for the game to thrive.

In high limit stud this doesn't happen. Because the progressive ante handicaps the best players and keeps the game looser, it also has the effect of maintaining a "proper balance of luck and skill." Therefore, the great players in the high limit stud games don't have any larger advantage over a "tourist" type player than a reasonably good player will at a limit like $15-$30.

The progressive ante compensates for their great skill, and thus the games thrive. This is why I say, "Detrimental is good."

Technical Ideas

Afterthought

As you can see, these mathematical ideas can and do impact your results significantly. Of course there is a lot more to poker than "just knowing the percentages," but the underlying mathematics of the game should not be neglected.

Those of you who scoff at this area will usually never be able to achieve expert status. Of course there are exceptions, but in my experience these exceptions actually do a much better job in this area than they would have you believe.

It's also interesting how some technical ideas, such as rake and structure can and do significantly impact your results at the poker tables. If only cardroom managers would become more knowledgeable in this area and begin to think more in the long term and less in the short term, we poker players would be better off. But we are not the only ones. The whole poker industry would also benefit greatly.

Part Three
Strategic Ideas

Strategic Ideas

Introduction

We have already addressed the idea that poker is easy to beat if you are only interested in making minimum wage. In fact, there are a few people who do just that. They play low limit games where the competition is very weak. They will "mooch" a few comps, and most important, they play very tight and straight forward which allows for the mathematics of their opponents' poor play to give them a little bit the best of it.

However, most people who take up poker seriously want to do better than this. They want to move into the middle limits where some real money can be won. But there is often a "small" problem when you try to do this and you stick to the formula of tight, straight forward play. It is the fact that many of your opponents now play reasonably well and they will adjust to your playing style and adjust to it quickly. Now instead of making minimum wage, you will slowly get "ground down."

Yet there are a small number of people who do quite well in these bigger games. These are the handful of experts who not only play tight, but have learned to play their hands well all the way through. This includes appropriate aggressiveness, the ability to trap, knocking out opponents on early rounds with second- and third-best hands, knowing how to maximize the probability of winning when the pot has become reasonably large, and making many other appropriate adjustments.

Many of these concepts can be grouped under the general heading of "Strategic Ideas." That is what this section is about. It examines some of the adjustments that you must make and which your opponents will make as the games get a little tougher.

Ace-Eight Suited
— Under the Gun

On the Internet gambling group, rec.gambling.poker, there was a post that caught my interest not too long ago. In it, the poster claimed that in a typical full handed hold 'em game, ace-eight suited was a slightly profitable hand if you were to raise with it, first in, "under the gun." That is, if you are first in from an early position, the poster claimed that this hand would be worth playing, but just marginally so, and that you should raise with it. (If my memory serves me correctly he stated that it was a loser if you just called.)

What caught my interest is that if you ask any good, experienced player he will tell you that playing the hand this way should cost you money in the long run. In addition, if you follow the advice that we give in *Hold 'em Poker for Advanced Players* you would normally throw this hand away, but might occasionally play it in a loose, passive game or in a moderately aggressive game that features two or three players who play virtually any ace.[10] However, if you play it you should normally only call. (I actually play it a lot when I am first in up front. But that's because I'm frequently in games that are loose enough, and will just call with it. However, unless you play very well on the flop and beyond, if you threw it away every time it can never theoretically cost you very much.)

So how did the poster arrive at his conclusion, and where did he go wrong? My understanding is that he took one of the better hold 'em simulators and programmed all his opponents to be reasonable players, and then played millions of computer generated hands, and saw that he was making a small profit. This

---

[10] See page 25 of *Hold 'em Poker for Advanced Players: 21st Century Edition.*

brought him to the conclusion that you should raise with ace-eight suited under the gun.

For the sake of argument, let's assume that he did everything right. That is the computer simulation that he ran does do a good job of representing real hold 'em, and that the typical players he programmed, did represent typical hold 'em players. Then it would appear that ace-eight suited is a raising hand when first in "under the gun," and that we should all be doing it.

Let's look a little deeper. Suppose I'm in a game, and an unknown player I don't know, raises under the gun, I am a couple of positions to his left, and no one else is in. Here's what I usually do. I reraise with a very small number of hands. These include aces, kings, queens, jacks, and sometimes tens. It also includes ace-king suited and offsuit. In addition, I call with an even smaller number of hands. These include ace-queen suited, ace-jack suited, and king-queen suited. (See our warning in *Hold 'em Poker for Advanced Players* about playing the ace-jack suited and king-queen suited in this spot.) And, most important, virtually all other hands are almost always thrown away. I know it sounds very tight, but that's how I usually play.

Here's what's interesting. Assuming this is my strategy, it would make sense for an under the gun player to raise with the ace-eight suited because I won't be there often enough to challenge him. That is, if I and others, are following a strategy such as described above, it would be proper for him to open up a little. (There are also other strategies that other players could be following that would also make it right for our under the gun player to play loose and aggressive.)

But suppose I begin to notice that this new player is an awfully loose raiser up front. He is willing to fire away with hands that I wouldn't be raising with, and many times wouldn't even play given that position. (This can include hands like ace-eight suited, medium suited connectors, medium to small pairs, and two unsuited medium high cards such as ace-jack and king-ten.) Well, when this happens, it is time to adjust by adding a few hands to play against him. They include ace-queen offsuit, nines, and eights, and I will always reraise with them.

Notice that the equation has now changed. If you have players behind you who are now playing in the above manner, those ace-eight suiteds that you have been raising with can now become expensive. Not only will you be forced to frequently play a marginal hand out of position for a lot of money, but you won't have as good a read on your opponent because of the expansion of hands that his reraise now represents.

I believe that this was the mistake that the poster made. I doubt very much if his simulations accounted for how other players, particularly the better ones (who also happen to be very observant) will adjust their play. I have found expert poker to be a game of constant adjustment. Those who do it best, along with all the other attributes that are required to become a top player are the ones that excel at the game.

Finally, to close this essay, there is one other concept worth pointing out. We have actually touched on it, and it is the idea that you should play a little too tight than seems proper if you are holding a hand that can easily get you in trouble if someone else plays.

Here's another example of this. In our book *Seven-Card Stud for Advanced Players* we caution that you should not steal every time, even if you are 100 percent certain of success. That is, you should still throw your very worst hands away. The reason for this is that you do not want your opponent to change his non-existent calling frequency in this situation. By not stealing quite as much as you could, your opponent may never realize that he should be defending a lot more.

As you can see, poker is a game of give and take. But what's interesting about this is that you should sometimes take a little less than what you could get in the short run to ensure that you can take the maximum in the long run.

Unusual Strategies

Imagine you're playing hold 'em; you pick up your cards and discover you hold two aces. Thrilled about achieving this 220-to-1 shot, you raise the blinds and watch everyone else fold. You're disappointed; but at least you won the blinds.

You keep playing, and over five hours later you discover that you have again managed to pick up two aces. This time, remembering your earlier fiasco, you just limp in. You want to do better than just winning the blinds.

Now eight people call, and when the smoke clears your two aces are beaten by someone who played two random cards. Not only do you feel a little sick, but you remember your earlier success when you won the blinds.

So, when is it best to limp or raise with two aces? Should you be trying to trap people or is it best to limit the field to maximize your chance of winning the pot (which may or may not maximize your expectation)?

I'm not going to answer that question. Partially because the answer is very complex and partially because the seemingly correct answer is not completely accurate. Let me be a little more specific...

Recently I saw a post on the Internet that I found incredibly interesting. Using a commercial hold 'em simulator, the poster showed that virtually no matter what quality of players his opponents were, his long run expectation was higher if he limped with aces under the gun, than if he raised. This was also true regardless of the playing strategy that he employed.

I have my doubts about this. In my experience, this would not be accurate. But as in the previous essay, for the sake of argument, let's assume that the results of the poster were reasonably accurate. That is, in most situations, when you are dealt two aces under the gun, you would be better off limping. Let's see if we can "blow a hole" in this assumption.

Suppose that at your hold 'em table there was a player who, in early position, not only played fairly tight but always limped with a big pair. That is, if he held aces, kings, queens, jacks, or tens up front he would just call the blinds. Thus, if he raises in this position, he must either have ace-king or ace-queen.

Now a hand appears where this person raises under the gun and you just happen to be on his immediate left. What should you do?

Your strategy is very simple. You should reraise no matter what your hand is, as long as it is likely that your reraise will get you heads up. On the flop you should almost always bet unless an ace flops. (The exceptions would be that you have flopped a slow playing hand or that you can beat aces when the ace comes.) You would have a large edge playing in this manner.

Of course, it would be very unlikely to ever find someone who played like this, but I think this example illustrates a point. If your strategy is such that the more observant and knowledgeable players can accurately narrow your range of possible hands (in their mind), you have a problem. This is because they will make adjustments to their playing strategy to counter-act your strategy, and these adjustments could prove to be quite expensive for you.

This is one of the reasons why I thought the poster's results were misleading. Even if the simulations were done accurately, they don't always show the whole story; however, statistical logic frequently will. When you are thinking about employing an unusual strategy to take advantage of your opponents, *you must also think about what unusual strategy they might use to take advantage of you.*

On the other hand, if you were against players who were either unaware or totally unfamiliar with your game, then an unusual strategy that narrows your possible hand can be quite profitable. But this might be the case only for a short period of time.

A Note on Slowplaying

Virtually everyone who reads this knows what slowplaying is. Generally, they will say something like, "You have made a very strong hand on an early round and are afraid that if you bet or raise you won't get any action, or will reduce the amount of action that you are entitled to. Thus, you should play your hand meekly in order to give your opponent a chance to catch up a little so that he can pay you off on a later street." In other words, you adjust your strategy away from the strength of your hand in an attempt to capture a few extra bets.

An obvious example of a slowplay from seven-card stud would be when you start off with rolled-up kings and a player on your right raises with a queen up, and you know that if you reraise, this person, and others, might throw their hand away. This should be an obvious slowplay. You should call, and you may want to check again on fourth street regardless of what you catch. (If you catch suited, you may want to bet to represent a flush, especially if your suit was live.)

But there is actually another reason to slowplay. It is not the fact that your decision not to bet or raise has little impact on your chances of winning the hand, but that it may increase the amount of money that you win (assuming you do win) when the hand is over. Notice that this is exactly the case with the three kings above. By only calling, you should win almost as often as if you had raised, assuming that your opponent will call your raise, but you may win a much bigger pot.

Here's another example. Instead of rolled-up kings, let's suppose you began with three fours, and there are several players still to act behind you. Now you should be much more inclined to reraise rather than call. This is because it is much easier to lose with a starting set of fours than a starting set of kings. In other words, your decision to slowplay in this situation is much more likely to affect the outcome of the hand, so you should be less

114

likely to do it. (Now I'm not saying that you should never slowplay in this spot. But I am saying you have something else to consider.)

Let's look at a different example. This time you are playing hold 'em and are dealt a pair of kings. Since you like this hand, you raise. Every one folds except the player in the big blind who calls. An ace flops and this person checks to you. Normally your play is to bet, and usually you will be quickly done with the hand if you get check-raised. It will now be too likely that you are against an ace, and with only two outs the pot needs to be huge for you to continue. (Of course many players do pay off in this spot, and in the long run it costs them plenty.)

But let's assume that you are against a very aggressive opponent who loves to check raise. In fact, you know that he is just as likely to make this play with middle pair as well as top pair, and then bet it all the way. When this is the case, you can't throw your hand away, and unless the board gets very scary, you'll pay off at the end. (You could argue that he is more likely to have played an ace than any other card, so that he is still a favorite to have aces. But when you consider the other money already in the pot, you must keep playing against this particular opponent.)

Notice that one of our criteria for slowplaying has been met. Your failure to bet will have little outcome on your chances to win the hand. Also, if your opponent does have aces you have saved a little money, but if he has middle pair you have lost a little money. This should roughly balance out.

But not betting the flop may do something else for you. It may allow you to win a bigger pot when your two kings is the best hand. This is because your check may encourage your opponent to bluff. You now may get him to make both a double size turn and river bet with a hand that he originally planned to throw away, and in the long run you come out way ahead.

So we see that slowplaying does not necessarily require a very strong hand for that particular situation. While having the "monster" is certainly nice, if your failure to bet or raise has little outcome on who wins the pot, but will occasionally allow you to win a much larger pot when your hand is good, it may be right to slow down with a seemingly questionable hand.

Hold 'em Starting Hands and Game Type

On our Internet forums there has been a great deal of discussion concerning hand values and the Sklansky Hand Rankings. Posters have questioned whether jack-ten suited is really better than king-ten suited, and whether king-queen offsuit is really better than ace-nine suited.

Recently a new idea has emerged. It is the idea that the hand rankings are very accurate in a typical Sklansky and Malmuth game, usually referred to as an S&M game, but not as accurate in other games. Of course, this leads us to another question, and that is: What is a typical S&M game? Well, as far as I know there is no typical S&M game. At least when David and I wrote our books, we weren't thinking in these terms.

On the other hand, there is no question that the value of a starting hand at limit hold 'em is affected by many things. These include the structure of the game, your position, the number of players in the pot, how much it costs to play, the quality of your opponents, your own playing skills, how your opponents perceive you, whether there is a maniac in your game, whether someone is steaming, and the type of game that you are in.

The purpose of this essay is to look at the type of game that you are in and the effect it has on the value of your starting hand. Of course, as already pointed out, when you are playing you should consider many other factors before you decide to fold, call, or raise. However, the type of game is significant and it should influence your starting hand decisions. For example, you might find yourself occasionally raising with a hand that you would normally fold.

If your strategy is to just look at your starting two cards and then to make a decision, you are not doing a very good job at the hold 'em table. It is true, especially if the rest of your game is fairly good, that you can still be a winning player with this approach, but you won't win what a true expert should. Furthermore, always playing on "automatic pilot" will not get the money against tough players. You need to make the appropriate adjustments.

Most players who do make some adjustments usually think in terms of the game being either loose or tight. They tend to play more hands in a loose game and are more selective in a tight game, especially from an early position. While there is no question that this is a better approach than just looking at your first two cards and then making your decision, it is still highly lacking. I recommend that you think in terms of four game types. They are as follows:

1. **Game Type No. 1: Loose and Passive.** This would be a game where there are many players in each pot, but very little raising. When someone bets or raises they almost always have a quality hand. There is very little bluffing and semi-bluffing, but a lot of calling, and the best hand almost always wins in the showdown. This is clearly the best type of poker game to be in. Unfortunately, they are few and far between.

2. **Game Type No. 2: Loose and Aggressive.** Not only are there many players in each pot, but there is much raising and some pots are capped. When someone bets, they frequently are merely representing a hand and many players are quick to raise with what appears to be a "second best hand." Furthermore, many players are quick to bluff or semi-bluff and you will often be getting large odds to make a call with a weak hand. In addition, you will frequently have to put in two or three bets to play on the flop and beyond. Even though these games can be highly profitable, they can also cause your bankroll to go through some large gyrations. Loose aggressive games are fairly common.

3. **Game Type No. 3: Tight and Passive.** You won't see many games like this, but they do occasionally exist. (They are more likely during the day when the regulars are out in

force.) Their characteristics are few players in each pot and very little betting or raising unless the hand warrants it. Many people think that these games are bad, but they can be more profitable than you think since your semi-bluffs can be very effective.

4. **Game Type No. 4: Tight and Aggressive.** This is clearly the worst type of poker game. The players will usually be playing quality hands, but will bluff and semi-bluff enough that you can never be completely sure. Furthermore, some of the players are quick to apply the pressure whenever they perceive weakness and it requires a highly skilled player to consistently beat these games.

I want to note that very few games will fall into exactly one of these categories. But these game types should play an important role in influencing your starting hand decisions.

So, as was previously stated, many players, when they think in terms of game type, think only in terms of loose and tight. They neglect the all important idea of passive versus aggressive which we will now address.

The major effect that passive/aggressive should have on your hand selection is the number of hands that you can play. Simply put, the more passive a game is, the more hands you can play. This is because it won't cost you much to play, and if you do get caught with a questionable hand there won't be a big penalty.

When the game becomes very aggressive you will usually have to wait for the premium hands. This is because the high implied odds that many hands require won't be there due to the large amount of money you will be initially required to put into the pot.

The major effect of loose/tight is on the mix of hands that you play. "Mix" refers to categories of hands such as small pairs, suited connectors, and unsuited high cards.

Many players think they can play more hands in a loose game. What they have done is confuse loose with "loose and passive." Playing many hands in a loose, but very aggressive game, can be suicide to your bankroll.

Let's now look at some specifics concerning starting hands by game type:

1. **Loose and Passive.** As mentioned previously, this is the ideal game and you can play many hands. The hands that move up in value the most when compared to the Sklansky Hand Rankings are the suited connectors. Not only will there be plenty of people in the pot to pay you off when you do make your hand, but when you flop a weak draw (such as a gut shot) you will often get a free or cheap card that allows you to continue playing.

2. **Loose and Aggressive.** The hands that move up most in value are the small pairs. When you flop a set you can be assured that many bets will go into the pot and your hand will be well concealed. Suited connectors don't do as well as many people think. The reason for this is that when you flop a weak draw you will frequently be bet out of the pot. (Think about the number of times that your gut shot got there, but you had already thrown your hand away.) Unsuited high cards lose value, but hands like any ace-suited, especially if the kicker is large, gain value because they have the ability to occasionally win a huge pot.

3. **Tight and Passive.** Here the unsuited high cards gain value. This is because one pair will frequently win, and your hand will sometimes win without improving. Medium pairs also go up in value. If an overcard flops, and someone bets, you don't have to guess as to whether you are beat — you can safely throw your hand away. On the other hand, small pairs and suited connectors usually lose value because they will not get the multiway action that they require. However, the connectors will frequently produce beneficial semi-bluff situations.

4. **Tight and Aggressive.** All hands lose value in this game simply because you are now in a game where many of your opponents are playing well. And it is difficult to win money

from people who are playing well. However, this said, those hands that need multiway action are usually (but not always) the type of hands hurt the most. These include small pairs, suited connectors, and hands like ace-little suited.

In addition, hands with questionable kickers go way down in value due to the pressure that better players can put on you. This is one of the reasons Sklansky ranks a hand like jack-ten suited, higher than king-ten suited (since the straight potential outweighs the pair potential), and the difference is most pronounced in a tight and aggressive game.

I again want to stress that the situation can change much of the above analysis. For example, even if the game is tight and aggressive, if a pot develops where several players have limped in and you are in a late position with a small pair, your hand has increased in value and you should get into that pot. On the other hand, if only one or perhaps two players had limped in, it might be correct to throw the small pair away. You won't be getting the right price to flop a set, and your opponents' semi-bluffs, along with their real bets, will only cost you money on the flops and beyond.

Finally, another reason to vary your strategy from what the game types usually call for is your particular opponent. If, for example, a loose, wild player raises, no one else is in, and it is now your turn, your main criterion in making whatever decision that you think is proper are your starting hand versus the range of hands that your opponent may hold. But if the decision is close, the game type should sway you one way or another.

Always Calling on the End

For years I have been counseling that in games like limit hold 'em or seven-card stud you should strive for a tight image. In these games the bet is often very small in relation to the size of the pot. This means that winning the pot is frequently much more important than gaining an extra bet. (I actually don't consider image to be a very important subject. If you play well your image should take care of itself. In other words it is a by product of your actions as opposed to an important thrust of your actions.)

Recently, I have several times seen the argument that the trouble with a tight image is that against players who tend to call too much, your tight image will only have the effect of making them play better. In other words, if someone is calling too much, and how they perceive you makes them call less, you might be turning a bad player into a good player. And I do agree that one of the things you want to do in poker is to make a weak playing opponent play worse, not better.

The other night I was sitting in a $15-$30 hold 'em game at The Bellagio. A hand came up that made me think of this argument. What happened was that I held a queen-eight offsuit in the small blind. Three people limped in and I threw in a $5 chip.

The flop came

and I bet. Now there's no question that this is a highly debatable bet, but it is not the purpose of this essay. It might be right for most players to check in this situation, but I threw my money in the pot and got two callers. A deuce came on fourth street, I bet and the first player called. A five came on the river and I checked.

Notice that there is very little reason for me to bet. Even though I might have the best hand, there is almost nothing that my opponent can call me with which will leave me with the best hand. If he has a king, I am beat. If he has a queen, his kicker will probably beat mine, and if he has a busted draw, he will just throw his hand away. But after my check, he surprised me and bet.

So the question is should I call or fold? Well, if you have been counting there are now seven big bets in the pot. That is, the pot is offering 7-to-1 on my call and if my opponent will bluff a little over 12 percent of the time, a call becomes correct.

My opponent was an unknown player. With the king-queen out there it seemed likely that someone would call down with a draw, so there was no way that middle pair should be thrown away. Hence I called. My opponent turned his hand over and showed an ace-ten. I had caught him bluffing and added seven big bets to my stack, which is a lot of chips in a game where the best players only do a little better than one big bet an hour. In other words, a fold on my part would be disastrous in this situation if my opponent is bluffing.

Now most of you will probably agree that this is a fairly uneventful hand. In fact, by hold 'em standards it is not even a very large pot. And if my strategy was just to call every time, no matter who I was against, it wouldn't be far from wrong.

But suppose that my opponent had a tight image. Let's say that it was common knowledge that he was the type that would virtually never bluff in this spot. If that was the case, my hand should be tossed and the bet on the end will be saved.

Now let's suppose I was wrong. Let's assume that the person who would supposedly never bluff (in this spot) because that is how I perceived him, actually works a few steals in. Then I will think I'm saving money by not paying off, but in reality it might be costing quite a bit.

This is precisely what I see happening in hold 'em all the time. The same comments can also be true in seven-card stud as long as you are playing at least middle limit. (That is $15-$30 or higher where the ante is at least reasonably large compared to the bets.) *When you take a player who normally calls a lot and get him to lay down a few hands on the end, you can be coming out way ahead.* I agree that if you get him to play less hands before the flop (and on third street in stud) you may be making him play better, but on the later streets this is certainly not the case.

So the next time you are contemplating about the "awful" tight image you have developed because you are trying to play well, just be aware that this image will make you a little bit of extra money against players who are somewhat aware, but don't understand how the size of the pot should impact their play. In fact, you should be pleased that some of your opponents consider you to be tight and unimaginative. Just make sure to occasionally work that bluff in when the situation calls for it. (Also, when that bluff is successful, never show it. If asked, just confirm that they were correct to fold and be prepared to make the play again.)

Raising with Suited Connectors

On our forums at www.twoplustwo.com there has been a great deal of discussion as to when it might be right to raise with a hand like

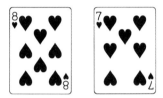

when playing limit hold 'em. To my surprise, this hand has created a great deal of debate so I thought that I would quickly summarize three such situations.

Situation No. 1: You are first in early. Suppose you hold a hand like 8♥7♥, are in early position, and no one (except the blinds) has yet to enter the pot. You generally should throw the hand away. The reason for this is that with many players still to act there can be much better hands behind you and you can find yourself playing short-handed for two or three bets with a hand that does poorly in this situation. This is because a medium suited connector usually requires high implied odds to do well in the long run.

But there is an exception. Suppose you are in a game that contains several observant players who will adjust their decisions based on their observations. Now if you play this hand up front — usually by coming in with a raise — your (observant) opponents will not give you credit for it. This will allow you to often steal the blinds and to surprise them if you make a hand. You may also be able to successfully bluff if a high card hits and no one else

125

makes anything strong. However, even though this play has value in the right spot, we don't recommend that you do it very often.

Situation No. 2: You are first in late. If no one (except the blinds) is in and you hold this hand in a late position you should usually raise. This will give you three possible ways to win. First, everyone remaining might fold and you will have captured the blinds. Second, you might get called but your bet (or bets) may allow you to steal on the flop (or a later street). (Be careful here. If you are called on the flop and keep betting, this hand can become quite expensive.) Or third, you might make the best hand and occasionally win a nice pot.

The reason I said "usually," is that it can be right to call if you are first in from a late position if you know that the remaining players, particularly those in the blinds, are very loose and that it is very likely your raise will not win the pot for you. The hand is worth playing cheaply against the two blinds and maybe the button, but isn't worth raising when there is no chance to steal the pot.

By the way, this hand is much better than two random cards when first in from a late position. First, if you make a pair you will beat anyone with ace high or a small pair. Second, in addition to being able to make pairs (or better) there are many draws that you can pick up. This fact alone allows you to semi-bluff more and occasionally win a pot.

Situation No. 3: You are in a late position, and many have already called the blind. In *Hold 'em Poker for Advanced Players* our advice is to occasionally raise with this hand. But this is not something that you do at random in an attempt to throw your opponents off even though it might have that effect if you hit your hand. Furthermore, it is not something that you should do at random. You do it when the situation is right.

Here's what we say in *Hold 'em Poker for Advanced Players: 21st Century Edition:*

"But we should point out that you need to consider your opponents before raising with a hand like 8♥7♥. If you are against players who not only play too many hands, but go too far with their hands regardless of the size of the pot, there is less value to raising. Part of the reason for making this raise is to entice your opponents to continue on if you happen to get a flop to your liking. But if you are fairly sure that they will do precisely that anyway, then you should usually just call."

In other words you need to consider the games that you play in. If you are a low limit player who frequently finds himself in the so called "no fold 'em hold 'em" games then you should just call when in this situation. On the other hand, if your game is a little tighter, and players require a little something to continue on after the flop then you should be inclined to give them that "little something" in the form of a bigger pot.

One final note. Even though we have been talking about when it might be right to raise with a hand like 8♥7♥, keep in mind that there are many other spots where it is best to just throw these hands away. If you are one of those people who automatically play this and similar hands, then in most games you will be giving up a lot. This is especially true when the game is aggressive.

Seven-Six Suited

Another debate that we have had on our Internet forums, deals with the merits of seven-six suited. The theory was put forth that in "ramming-jamming" games you are actually better off for your hand not to be suited. This way you will avoid losing a flush over flush confrontation, and be able to easily get away from your hand. Of course this argument is ridiculous.

To see exactly how ridiculous it is, all you have to do is pretend that your hand is not suited and play it as such. Now your seven-six suited will do exactly as well in those situations where it is appropriate to play a seven-six offsuit (and there aren't very many of these) as long as no flush comes into play. But occasionally you will discover that you have made a flush on the river and have collected some extra money with the hand. So if you choose to follow this strategy there is no question that you would prefer to have this hand suited no matter what the game type.

With this being the case, let's take a closer look at seven-six suited. Specifically, let's address the question "Should we be playing this hand in a wild game?" In other words, how does the ramming jamming affect the value of this holding?

To answer this question, we must understand that small suited connectors are hands with no immediate value. What I mean by this is that it is virtually impossible to win a pot with a seven high. Compare this to a hand that contains an ace where through the strength of this high card it sometimes wins the pot on the river without any improvement.

What this means is that a hand like

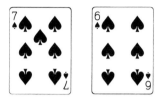

requires odds. You want to get in as cheaply as possible and be pretty sure that no one else will raise, (although you may want to raise yourself if many limpers come in in front of you in case you get lucky and do make a hand).

Here's a couple of simple examples. Suppose you are first in early. Do you play? The answer is no. You cannot be sure that there won't be one or more raises behind you. (The exception would be an extremely passive game. But they are quite rare now-a-days.)

Suppose you are in a late position, but the pot has been raised. Would it be correct to call here? The answer is again no. Although if there were also several callers you should probably play, but even then it's close. If your suited connector was higher, such as

the call might be correct. Now you can not only make a bigger flush (or straight) but also a bigger pair. Notice that catching a winning pair is much more likely with a jack or a ten than a seven or a six. Thus, the larger suited connector is significantly more valuable.

So, as we can see, the time to play a hand like seven-six suited is when you can get in cheaply, are fairly sure that there won't be any other raising, and that there are already several players in. This means that you can profitably call a bet from late position in an unraised pot if several players are already in, or you can call for one bet out of the big blind if it is raised. (You can also play if first in, late, as a steal.)

Now suppose you are in a wild game. By this I mean a game where almost every pot is raised and many of the hands go to three bets or more preflop. How does this affect the small suited connector? It means that you should hardly ever play it. When you do play it, it will be because the earlier criteria has been met. That is, for some reason the game has calmed down (for this hand) and you can get in for one bet against multiple opponents and are either in the blind or in late position (or perhaps receive a free play out of the blind).

Put another way, you won't be concerned that your hand is suited in a "ramming-jamming" game since you will usually throw it away. However, when you do play it, the fact that it is suited makes all the difference.

Now let's address the question of making a flush and losing to a higher flush. This will, on occasion, happen. There is no denying that. But if you follow the above guidelines it won't happen very often, and in my experience it is a fairly rare event. It is true that you will sometimes make a flush on fourth street only to have a fourth suited board card come on the river, but those are just the breaks and are part of the game. Again, if you follow the above guidelines you will be in there in the right situations with this hand.

On occasion however, you'll flop a flush draw and there will be a great deal of action indicating that another flush draw is out there. When this happens it almost always means that the other flush draw is higher than yours, and you should simply fold. Again, this won't happen very often, but when it does there is no need to throw good money after bad.

Finally, there is one type of otherwise good player who does lose money with this hand. It is someone who is aware that the better players can play a few more hands, thinks he is one of them, and thus plays these small suited connectors in many of the situations outlined above where we have just concluded that they are losers. For this person, having the small connector suited is a detriment.

Art and Science

The other day I made a very simple play, which earned a couple of bets on the river, that many of you would not make. On the button, my hand was a small set, and when a third spade hit (on the end) there was no hesitation in my bet and two players paid off. The key to this bet was simple hand reading which made it clear that there was no flush out. So all I had to do was bet and see what it collected.

The reason this play was so simple to make was that everyone checked the flop and that there was no raise before the flop. Thus, there was no reason to "check to the raiser," and if anyone had flopped a flush draw, any of these players would have bet the flop. So even though the scare card came, there was virtually no way that it could be truly scary and a bet could only collect more money.

David Sklansky and I have written that reading hands is both an art and a science. But in my opinion the science aspect far outweighs the art. Many of you will disagree with this, arguing that to read hands well you need to have a good feel for the game. I won't dispute this. But I counter that "good feel of the game" really means knowing your opponents tendencies and also having an excellent understanding of the appropriate underlying concepts that govern expert play. You then must combine this with one or more key events in the play of the hand to zero in on what an opponent is likely to hold.

Here's an example of a hand I recently played in a $30-$60 hold 'em game at The Bellagio. I raised under the gun with the

and was reraised by a late position player. I called and the two of us looked at a flop of

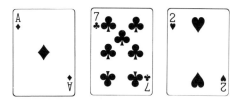

I promptly check raised my opponent who only called. The 3♣ hit on the turn. I bet and was raised. Before continuing, let's pause and consider my opponent's hand. Well, what was it?

Based on the information given, you can't be sure. You need to consider your opponent. A conservative player would either have two aces or ace-king (like me). There is nothing else that he can have. So against this opponent, all I have is a "crying call."

But what if my opponent is the loose aggressive type. Given the board, there is another hand that he could have, and it is ace-queen suited. Now he would frequently three bet before the flop, get the raise in on fourth street, and be willing to check it down on the river.

Notice that my hand is much better than a crying call since it can beat two of his possible hands. Namely

and

(Note that he can't have A♥Q♥ or A♦Q♦ since those two aces are already accounted for.) He can also have

which beat me, or 6 combinations of ace-king since there are two aces and three kings left. This means that on the turn I am actually the favorite in terms of money to be won since I hold the best hand twice as often as my opponent does. We tie the rest of the time. However, if a queen or a club comes on the river, it's back to the crying call situation.

As you can see, in a sense this hand requires much "feel" because my judgement of my opponent needs to be very accurate. That's the art part. But with experience and a good deal of hard study and thinking about the games, this "art" sort of turns to science. An expert hold 'em player can be very precise in these situations, where a lessor player will just become confused and mistake prone.

Changing the subject slightly, there is a particular player I know who spends a great deal of time trying to convince people that he is a true expert. When he stepped up to the larger games he did very poorly and he now seems to be playing less and less.

So what was the reason for his failure, (which may only be temporary because he is smart enough to regroup)? It is precisely this area. His reading skills, which as far as I can tell he has never emphasized, left him behind those top players who could put him on a hand much more accurately than he could them. Thus, he played at a great disadvantage only to discover that perfect play on the first two cards and an understanding of aggressive strategic concepts isn't enough.

This is one of the reasons that I have always recommended starting at the small limits and working your way up. Reading hands is an area that is absolutely crucial to becoming an expert. But it doesn't come quickly and requires much effort over a long period of time. And, this more than any other reason, is why there are so few true experts at hold 'em (and other forms of poker).

Finally, for those of you interested, I lost the hand in question. A club came on the river and my loose aggressive opponent showed me the

So much for art and science.

Three Examples

Continuing with the theme of reading hands, what follows are three examples of hands from the $30-$60 game at The Bellagio where this skill played an important role in my decision making. It also needs to be pointed out that if you change slightly the assumptions made about some of my opponents, the correct strategy might be very different from what will be given below.

Example No. 1: Betting the best hand. This play was very simple and my hand should be bet all the time. What happened was that three typical players limped in and my holding was

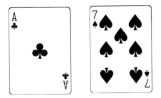

in the big blind, so I got a free play. The flop came

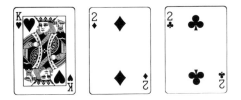

It should be clear to most of you that a bet on my part is almost always correct. The reason for this is related to how a typical player plays in this game. First, if they hold a king in their hand they will be more prone to raise if they do play. Second, notice that typical players, while they frequently play too many hands, are still less inclined to play a hand that contains a deuce because they are aware that low cards like deuces or treys have little value.

Thus, there is a good chance that my A♣7♠ is the best hand, and I don't want to give a free card so that someone can catch a pair to beat me. Of course if someone calls (or raises) my opinion may quickly change. (By the way, it may be right to bet *any* two cards in the above situation for similar reasons. The only advantage to A♣7♠ is that you may draw out on a king or pocket pair or may beat or tie someone else who calls with an ace on the river.)

Example No. 2: Betting for value. In this example, a weak player, in the sense that he played in a very straightforward manner, limped in under the gun. Another player called from a late position, I held

in the small blind and raised. The player in the big blind folded, and the two active opponents both called.

The flop came

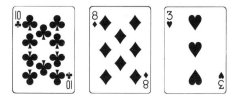

I bet; the under the gun player called, and the other player folded. Right here some conclusions can immediately be drawn from reading hands. Being straight forward, it is unlikely that my opponent has a ten, since he would have probably raised on the flop. So likely hands are either an eight giving him middle pair, or something like jack-nine or queen-jack for a draw. (Notice that since two queens are in play the queen-jack hand is less likely.)

The turn card looked very scary. It was the A♦. But again, this was a straight forward player who, if he played an ace in early position, would have been likely to raise. (Otherwise, if his hand contains an ace and he chooses not to raise, he would probably fold.) So again I have a fairly safe bet even though to many players the ace will look scary.

The river was the T♦. This card also looks scary, and there is no question that it is a little, since if my opponent has a draw, it may also be two suited diamonds. However, based on my earlier conclusion, it does not look like I am against three tens. Thus, if it is likely that my opponent will call again with a pair of eights, assuming that he holds one in his hand, I should probably bet again, even though there is a small chance I have run into a backdoor flush.[11]

Example No. 3: Checking to the aggressive raiser. This hand was also fairly straight forward. A loose-aggressive player raised from middle position. Even though he wouldn't raise on any two cards, there is no question that he would raise with a fair number of hands. Two players called behind him and I called from the big blind with

---

[11] It should be noted that sometimes it can be a major mistake to stick to your initial conclusions when attempting to put an opponent on a particular hand. Even though that was not the case here, subsequent action on a later round can and should influence your decision making process.

The flop came

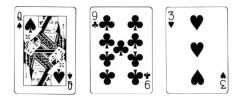

My play was to check, see what happens, and then make a decision. This is because most loose-aggressive players will bet virtually every time with this flop, assuming that they were the before the flop raiser. If he has top pair (or better) he will certainly bet, and if he can't beat queens, he will still bet hoping that no queen is out and that he might win the pot uncontested. (By the way, that strategy in this situation is probably correct due to the pot odds that he is getting. But that is not the point of this essay.)

As expected, the loose aggressive player bet and one of the players behind him called. Not only is the pot offering 10-to-1, but I was fairly sure that the player who called behind him would have raised if he held a queen. This means that there was a decent chance that my hand was best.

Thus, I should call and then make a decision as how to proceed depending on what the turn brings. For example, if an ace comes, it might be time to check and fold (to a bet). If a small card comes, my best play may be to lead at the pot. Furthermore, there is always a chance that I will catch a perfect card and collect from my opponents. (By the way, for those interested, another nine did come and I was paid off by the player behind the loose aggressive raiser.)

The Two Types of Stud

Generally, when you go to a cardroom you have three types of poker to choose from. They are Texas hold 'em, which we just refer to as hold 'em, seven-card stud, and finally, seven-card stud. All three forms are played limit. That is no-limit and pot-limit games are generally not available.

Now wait a minute. I know what you're going to say. You have just noticed that seven-card stud is listed twice. Well, that's not a mistake. It turns out that there are two types of seven-card stud. They are the kind where the initial ante is small compared to the bets, and the kind where the initial ante is (relatively) large in relation to the betting. How these types differ will be the focus of this essay.

Almost all of the first type is played at the smaller limits. This includes the small spread limit games such as $1-$5 which are usually played without an ante, but with a small bring-in, up to $10-$20 where the ante is usually $1 and the bring-in is $2. Most of us refer to this game as "little stud." It features small pots and very tight play by those who beat it.

But things change at the $15-$30 level. The ante is now $2 and the bring-in is $5. This calls for a completely different game. We refer to games at $15-$30 and above as "real stud."

Now before we continue, I'm aware that some players out there who play the small limit stud games aren't very happy with my use of the term "little stud." They say that they enjoy the game, that they win at it, and that it requires a fair amount of skill.

No one should argue with any of this. But it is usually a game of small pots, is not as skillful as the middle and high limits, and does not require the "courage" necessary to be a consistent winner. Thus, I believe that the terms little stud and real stud are appropriate. However, let me state that if your game is little stud and you do well at it, you have nothing to be ashamed of.

So what's the difference between little and real stud? Why is real stud more skillful? And, where does this idea of courage come in? Furthermore, since the only difference between some forms of little stud when compared to real stud is essentially the ante, how can this one change make that much of a difference? And finally, if real stud requires more skill than little stud, are they even the same skills? That is, are the skills that make a winning player at little stud the same skills that will allow someone to win at real stud? Let's take a look.

First, little and real stud differ in the general thrust of correct strategy. Little stud is essentially a trapping game, while big stud is usually a game of knocking people out. Of course there are some exceptions, but in little stud, since you start off with very little money in the pot, it's not necessary to steal the antes as often, and you are frequently trying to entice the weaker players into the pot. For example, suppose your starting hand is a pair of kings with a king up. In little stud you should frequently limp in for the bring-in or make less than a maximum bet in a small spread limit game. The idea is to trap a weak player, and then hope that by fourth street he has enough of a hand to stay with you. Of course you may get beat, but being able to take a big pair up against a smaller pair is a big advantage in this game.

In real stud, a pair of kings is almost always a raising or reraising hand. Yes, I know that there are some exceptions, and there may be times where you would like to trap someone by just limping. But you also need to steal the antes fairly often (unless the game is very loose and you know that you are very likely to be called). Many times when you have a king up and raise, you won't necessarily have a pair of kings. You might have a pair in the hole, a three flush, three big cards, or worse. Thus, you will need to balance many of the marginal raises with some legitimate raises, thus, making a pair of kings with a king up almost always a raising hand.[12]

---

[12] There may also be times where due to the number of players in the pot, your position in relation to the bring-in, the

This only partly addresses the issue. Not only is third street played much differently, but the upcards become much more important in real stud. As we show in our books, the upcards on board have the ability to change the value of a hand and can dramatically change the way that a hand should be played. But this is much more true for real stud than it is for little stud. This is because the size of the pot (relative to the size of the bet) is generally much larger at real stud. That is what appears to be a small change in the value of a hand can be very significant in real stud, but not in little stud.

Here's an example. At little stud if you believe that you are against a likely big pair, and on fifth street all you have is a small pair and a three flush, you should fold (unless the pot is quite large). It's as simple as that. In real stud, if your cards are live, and this includes your flush cards, as well as your trip cards and possible (two) pair cards, it may very well be right to continue. In addition, if your opponents upcards are not very live, it is frequently correct to continue chasing to the river. As you can see, there is a great deal of skill in real stud, and in my opinion the best poker players in the world are the great stud players.

So where does courage come in? Well as we just saw, you usually shouldn't chase very much in little stud. If you are fairly sure you don't have the best hand and your hand has little potential, you should usually get out. You just won't win enough to make it worth the expense.

But this isn't always the case in real stud. There may be enough money in the pot to keep playing. Furthermore, your overall expectation may be higher if you can get a third person to fold. This means that it is frequently right to raise what you think is best hand with the second best hand to get the third best hand to fold. It may also be right to raise with the third best hand to get the second best hand to fold. It takes a lot of courage to make these plays since they will usually seem to fail. That is the other

---

liveness of your hand, the exact rank and suit of your kicker, etc., your pair of kings is only worth a call.

player still comes or you succeed in getting him out, but you still lose the pot, and you have put in an extra bet.

As we can see, I have only touched the surface. The change in the (relative) size of the ante does make a big difference. Going from little to real stud requires an adjustment from a passive, tight game, where you are taking few chances, to an aggressive, moderately loose one where you are frequently willing to put a lot of chips in the pot.

But real stud requires much more. This includes great hand reading skills which take into account the upcards and the ability to parlay this skill into winning plays. This can include a timely bluff as well as an appropriate raise to either knock someone out or get more money in the pot. And it includes the ability to make some calls with very weak hands knowing that you will lose the majority of the time.

It should be obvious that the skills required to be successful are different between the two games. I don't believe that you can put an excellent little stud player into a large real stud game and expect him to be a favorite. Not only will he have trouble adjusting to playing at the higher limit, he won't have the proper skills to be successful.

Finally, I play both real stud and hold 'em. In may ways I think that real stud is the best game that a cardroom offers and highly recommend it. But I also recognize that little stud is a great game as well. If you are good at it, you might want to think about learning some additional skills and moving up to the middle and high limits. For most of you who are successful at little stud, working on these skills and moving up should be worth the effort.

Which is Better?

Suppose you're playing $30-$60 seven-card stud (with a $5 ante and a $10 bring-in). Your opponent is dealt:

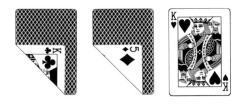

and you hold:

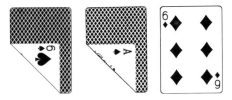

Which hand is better? (Before reading any further, make sure you come up with an answer and if possible, why you think that is the case. Then compare to what I write below.)[13]

First, if we were to run a hot and cold simulation, that is we just deal all the cards out, we see that the pair of kings will win just over 56 percent of the time and the pair of sixes with the ace kicker (and two flush) will win just under 44 percent of the time. What's interesting about this match up is if we ignore the bet on the end, which is usually favorable to the player with the small pair (less so if you are against a very tricky opponent), that player expects to break even in the long run providing that a bet is put

---

[13] Also note that at small limit seven-card stud some of the conclusions of this essay might be different due to the smaller ante structure.

into the pot on every street regardless of what the boards look like.

The reason you only need to win 44 percent of the time to break even is because of the additional $50 that is in the pot in antes and bring-in. However, we play poker to win money, not to break even. So to play this hand it must have playing advantages. Well does it?

To answer this question let's notice a couple of things that can happen. (Again, I assume that you hold the 6♠A♠6♦ and your opponent has the K♣5♦K♥.) First, if your opponent makes an open pair which may or may not be his door card, you usually fold. If you make an open pair, he will always stay with you if it is not your door card, and will often come if it is your door card. So we immediately see that you are not as likely to put a bet in on every round as your opponent is. Thus, you save money in many situations where he doesn't.

Second, who says that your opponent will bet every round? Many players, if they are unimproved on sixth street, won't always bet. Thus, instead of putting in $180 ($30 on third street, $30 on fourth street, $60 on fifth street, and $60 on sixth street) to see the river, it will sometimes only cost you $120 to do so.

Third, you may be able to buy yourself a free card. For instance, if he bets on fourth street, you might raise, and then on fifth street, if he checks, you can check after him. Here again, you are putting less than $180 in the pot to see the river.

And fourth, if you catch an ace you will have an opportunity to go for a check raise, which can be very profitable against the right player — usually a very aggressive one — while it will be much tougher for him to make the same play, because he will not be as confident that your hand will be good enough to bet.

So what do we have? We see that if you and your opponent were to automatically put a bet into the pot on each betting round, regardless of the boards, you only expect to break even. But we also see that poker isn't played that way, and the hand that at first appears to be weaker, has many playing advantages. So are these advantages enough for the 6♠A♠6♦ to catch up?

Well, I don't know for sure, and it would of course depend on exactly who you were against, since some players are easier to maneuver and less aggressive than others. But my guess is that in a heads-up situation the two hands play about even in terms of expectation. However, once other players come in, the small pair drops off in value. That's why we tell you in *Seven-Card Stud for Advanced Players* to do what it takes to get heads-up with a hand like this when the opportunity presents itself.

(For those interested, part of the reason why the small pair loses value is that many of your wins against the big pair come from making small two pair and small two pair does not do very well in multiway pots. *That is your probability of winning the pot is going down faster than the size of the pot is going up.*)

In closing, we see another example that there is much more to poker than it at first appears. Even though the rules that govern play are very simple, the game itself and the subtleties that it contains makes play fascinating and sometimes very unpredictable. I suspect that most of you would have thought that the pair of kings was the better hand, and the rest went for the pair of sixes. I bet that very few of you went for the idea that there wasn't much difference.

If you would like to do some more thinking on this subject try comparing the same K♣5♦K♥ to:

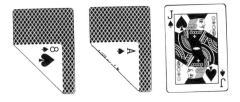

Strategic Ideas

Afterthought

Let's take a quick "re-look" at two of the essays, "Starting Hands and Game Type," and "Unusual Strategies." These essays are worth a little more examination because they address two of the traps that many relatively new players fall into.

There is no question that proper starting hand selection is very important. In fact, whether your game is stud or hold 'em, if you do a poor job in this area, you *must* lose. There is no way around it.

The trap is that some players begin to put too much emphasis on it, and thus, only play mediocre after the first round. In my opinion, if you strive to play the middle limits, this dooms you to be roughly break even in hold 'em and to only being a small winner in stud — you will probably only win one-third to one half what a true expert would.

The other trap has to do with playing poker the way we would like to play it as opposed to playing it the way that expert play requires. In his book, *The Psychology of Poker,* Alan Schoonmaker points out that "tight and aggressive" is learned behavior as opposed to natural behavior. It would be so much more fun to routinely come up with creative unexpected strategies that just devastate our opponents, and then watch our chip stacks grow. Unfortunately, good solid poker doesn't work that way. It requires much diligence and a complete understanding of the game.

Part Four

In the Cardrooms

In the Cardrooms

Introduction

All of my *Poker Essays* books contain a section called "In the Cardrooms." There is good reason for this. It is simply the fact that I find playing poker in many locations to be a frustrating experience. Dealing with unhappy players can be tough enough, but when these problems are compounded by cardroom procedures and hostile managerial attitudes it can be almost unbearable.

Now I have just used some very strong language in stating an opinion. Fortunately, the above does not apply everywhere. A few cardrooms today are well run, and many others are improving. Put another way, the adversarial relationship that frequently develops between the regular players and cardroom management is beginning to break down in many locations and has been solved in others.

This section will be another look at some of these ideas and hopefully will be helpful in making the poker experience better for both players and those people who work in our poker rooms. As the industry continues to attempt to grow, it can only be successful if poker rooms are well run on a day-to-day basis.

Comments on Collusion

At a recent BARGE gathering here in Las Vegas, David Sklansky and I gave a one hour question and answer session.[14] One of the questions we were asked had to do with cheating, and collusion in particular. David gave a detailed answer which I thought would interest everyone, so I am going to summarize it here.

Before I start, a little background should be given. Over the past few years there have been many posts on the Internet concerning this topic. This includes not only the user group rec.gambling.poker, but also our web page forums at www.twoplustwo.com. Needless to say, there are many different opinions on the subject, and many players, particularly those relatively new to poker, are quite anxious regarding possible cheating problems.

Specifically, the form of cheating that most poker players fear the most is collusion. This is when two or more players get together, and through a predetermined set of signals, play their hands differently from the way they normally would in an attempt to increase their profits. What follows is a short recap of David's comments on this subject.

First you need to understand that two people colluding is not that strong. This is because one needs to help the other, and there just aren't enough times when both players will be in a position to do that. So for collusion to work well you need a team of three or four people.

Second, you can't do anything real obvious. Experienced players will quickly pick up on any hands that are not played

---

[14] For those who don't know, BARGE stands for Big August Rec.Gambling Extravaganza, and it is a group of Internet poker players/gamblers who come to Las Vegas every summer to meet, play some poker, and have a good time.

normally, or in which something unusual happens. The idea of putting a player in the middle and trapping him for many raises will be quickly identified by other players at the table and cannot last for any reasonable length of time.

Therefore, unless the cheaters are very good players, they will *still* lose because colluding can only add a small amount to their profits. Also, they would have to trust each other for the rest of their lives to remain silent.

Another point is that they would be forced to constantly play in bad games since they can't all change to the better game, and they would make less money scamming a bad game than they would make on their own with the freedom to move around. And finally, you as a player would normally be avoiding games with them anyway, because with so many good players at the *same* table you would usually be choosing a different game.

Now none of this is proof that collusion is not going on somewhere, but it does imply that if you are an unscrupulous person, you are probably making a *mistake* by joining a partnership. And, since it would be a mistake to join a partnership (even if you are unscrupulous), you have to assume that other good players wouldn't make that mistake either.

Again, I want to point out that this doesn't apply as much when there is only one game in town because now it doesn't look as funny when the same players are always at the table. Furthermore, a mild scam can never be caught because it virtually never involves putting someone in the middle. If you are an excellent player, any extra edge will only add to your profits, but putting someone in the middle is too obvious and an excellent player would understand this and rarely try it.

Finally, I'd like to add some thoughts of my own. I have been playing poker consistently since the early eighties and I don't believe that I have ever run into this type of collusion problem.

(This includes the old player dealt games in Gardena, California). I'm not saying that it never happens, but I do believe that it is very rare, especially at the middle limits where I have spent most of my time.

I do believe that if you were playing in high limit games twenty-five years ago you probably would have run into problems. But fortunately those days are over.

Part of the reason for this is that cardroom management has learned that once their room gets a cheating reputation, whether it is deserved or not, it is only a matter of time before their business is doomed. This is one of the reasons that I have recommended to cardrooms not to spread pot limit or no limit games on a regular basis. In a game where someone can and will occasionally lose all their money on the turn of a card, it is inevitable that cheating accusations will materialize.

Another reason why cheating is not widespread as some of the claims represent, is that the players "police the game." I'm an experienced player, and I'm usually in a game with several other experienced players. If something "funny" were to happen, one of us would quickly pick it up.

So, this essay should almost bring a halt to the fears that some of you have. However, I do advise that you remain forever vigilant. When playing poker you should always be paying attention. This is not only good for your game in that it will help you make strategy decisions better, but it is good for everyone's game since it helps to assure that the poker games are "squeaky clean," and well run in every aspect.

Keeping Poker Honest

The biggest enemy of poker is cheating. Many people are quite concerned about it. Over the years, I have seen many cardrooms collapse and go out of business. I believe that some of these closures are due to the fact that these cardrooms developed a cheating reputation. Now this may surprise some of you since on many occasions I have argued that the games I play in are very clean. I have taken much criticism for this stance on cheating, but believe it to be the case. I try to call things as I see them. However, one thing is certain. Once a poker room acquires a cheating reputation, it is simply a matter of time before it becomes severely damaged. And this is the case whether the reputation is deserved or not.

There are many mechanisms present in cardrooms that help to keep the games honest. These include well-trained dealers, knowledgeable floor personnel, knowledgeable management, and modern security systems (which include surveillance cameras) to name a few. There is, however, another force at work in all cardrooms which plays an extremely important role in keeping the games clean. It is simply the fact that the players play independently of each other, and thus help to police the games themselves.

When I play, there are usually several experienced players at the table. Of course, with luck there will be some weak players as well, but these experienced players serve a very important role. They watch the game. It is hard to imagine that hands could come down "funny" in which these players would not recognize something was wrong. Again, *they police these games because they are playing totally on their own and are only interested in their own results.*

Let me give a simple example of how partnerships can change things. Suppose three players are in the pot. Furthermore, suppose that Player A bets, and after he is done betting the pot is offering Player B 3-to-1 on a 4-to-1 one shot. (That is, Player B will win 20 percent of of the time). Notice that Player B should fold, since his expectation is negative. Also, suppose that Player C is in the same situation, except that the cards required to make his 4-to-1 shot are completely different from those that Player B needs. (A possible example would be when each player has a flush draw on the river and their suits are different.) He too should also fold because he has negative expectation.

Now suppose that Players B and C are partners and are playing from the same bankroll. Notice that instead of each of them getting 3-to-1 to call, the team is getting 3-to-2 since the initial size of the pot stays the same. But also notice something else, instead of each of them individually having a 20 percent chance of winning, the team now has a 40 percent chance of winning, and 40 percent is exactly the same as 3-to-2. So in this example we see that the partnership has greatly benefitted them.

Again, I have very few worries about this sort of thing in the regular games. That is because virtually all participants play independently and we all do our job of policing the games.

As most of you know, my time at the poker tables is spent mainly in side games. Occasionally you can find me in a tournament, but it is only occasionally. Part of the reason for this is that I feel the independence of players is frequently violated. There are many practices in tournaments which are common place, which virtually never happen in the standard ring games. These include deal-making, players trading pieces of each of other, players buying pieces of other players, and players being staked — some of whom have long-term staking deals.

My fear is two-fold. First, these arrangements should have the effect of weakening the independence between players that poker (and tournament poker) must have to help assure that the games stay totally honest. Second, I feel that as these arrangements become more common place and more people become comfortable with them, they will spill over into the ring games. This will have the effect of damaging the cardrooms and poker in the long run.

(I am aware that in some of the very largest games, where only a very small number of people participate, players do take pieces of each other. However, when this is done it is usually announced to everyone at the table and all players have the option to object.)

So it appears to me that tournaments need to make efforts to clean up these practices. With that in mind, here are some suggestions which are targeted mainly for tournament directors, but which all of us should be aware of:

1. **All deal-making needs to be stopped.** Most tournaments are top heavy in their payout structure, which causes players to want to make a deal towards the end when the betting limits tend to be very high relative to the number of chips left on the table. Payout structures should be flattened, and the incentive for making the deals will be over.

2. **Players should not be allowed to trade pieces with each other, nor should they be allowed to buy pieces of other players.** Of course this may be difficult to implement, but one way to help accomplish this could be through peer pressure, and having tournament participants sign an oath, pledging themselves to be playing totally independently of other players in the tournament.

3. **Tournament directors should talk to those individuals who are known to stake more than one player in the same tournament, and ask them not to do so.**

Another point which should be especially important to tournament players, is the idea that as long as these practices are known to be widespread it is hard to imagine any legitimate national company coming in as a sponsor. The potential for scandal and perceived improprieties is just too great.

The poker world is often divided into two groups. The tournament players and the non-tournament players. Of course there are many individuals who participate in both areas, and that is just the point. To assure that poker stays honest, which will allow it to grow and expand, all aspects of poker must be "squeaky clean." It is hard to imagine poker being this way without all players who participate, no matter what form that participation takes, playing totally independent of each other. This is not something that should be taken lightly; and to achieve this goal many of you would have to make some sacrifices. In the short run, some of you who are getting free rides in these tournaments will have to pay your own way; some of you who are reducing your fluctuations by selling or trading pieces of yourselves will just have to live with higher swings; and some of you who are making a living at the tournaments may find it tougher to do because your income will be less consistent. But for the long-term good of poker it needs to be done and it needs to be done now.

Finally, I'm well aware that what is being proposed will not happen in totality. It is hard to imagine many poker players who are willing to accept a short term disadvantage for the long term good of poker. But if nothing else, I believe that what I have proposed should at least be the *official stance* of tournaments in order to give them the same degree of legitimacy that other sports tournaments have.

Talking Dealers

I've played a lot of poker over the years in many locations, at many different limits, and all different games. Of course I'm not the only person who can make this claim. There are many of us who have been around a long time. Some have played much more than me. But I believe that we all have one thing in common. We are all dissatisfied with the quality of many poker dealers. In fact, some people who have played poker for a long time will tell you that they "Have had it with bad dealers."

Over the years many articles have been published about player abuse towards dealers. There's no question that this is true, and it is more pronounced at the higher limits. But what is rarely mentioned is that in many instances, even though the player is overreacting, the dealer caused the initial problem.

I believe that a large percentage of the problems that occur in a cardroom can be directly attributed to dealer incompetence. Now to be fair, the majority of dealers do a pretty good job, and some dealers are actually quite good. But there are enough bad ones that at times it can drive you crazy. And it's not just here in Las Vegas. With the growth of poker there needs to be more quality dealers.

Bad dealers not only hurt the players, they hurt the cardroom, and they certainly hurt the competent dealers. Most dealers will tell you that when they follow certain dealers in the lineup, their tips are significantly off and the players are tougher to deal with. So you see, everyone benefits from top quality dealers.

So how can this problem be solved? What exactly causes the problem? In my experience the vast majority of dealing problems are caused by one thing. The dealer spends much of his time in the box talking. When they do this they aren't focused on the game as well as they should be. They deal too slow. They make a lot of errors. They irritate some of the players who aren't interested in their conversation. And, when a dispute occurs they don't do a good job of describing the events. All of this because the dealer was trying to be part of the game instead of the professional they should be.

To drive my point home, some of the worst situations that I have seen at a poker table occur when there is a dispute and the dealer's description of what happened is not even close to what actually happened. In truth, to cover the fact that they were talking (or otherwise not paying attention), they describe the events in such a way that it becomes someone else's fault instead of their own. Needless to say this makes the situation worse.

Excessive dealer talking is an industry wide problem. But there are a couple of cardrooms in California that have successfully addressed this problem — they do not allow their dealer's to converse. And when I visited these two cardrooms the games were great, and I can't help but think that their high quality dealing staffs had a lot to do with it. Many other cardrooms have this no extraneous conversation rule on their books, but enforcing it has proved difficult.

One of our books written by Dan Paymar, Donna Harris, and myself is called the *Professional Poker Dealer's Handbook*. Here is an excerpt from the introduction to the first chapter.

You, the poker dealer are a very important member of this team. You must be able to work successfully with your fellow dealers, the other cardroom personnel, and the players to whom you deal the cards to. You must also keep in mind the objectives of the casino, the cardroom, and your customers. But most important of all, you must pay strict attention to the game at hand and do your job quietly and efficiently.

Many dealers claim their job is a difficult one. Most players feel that anyone can be a competent dealer. We recognize that becoming a competent and efficient dealer is not easy. However, we do believe that with the proper attitude and effort there is no excuse for not becoming a *professional*. In this way, a dealer's job can be a rewarding one.

Cardroom Problems

I spoke at The World Poker Conference in 1998 that was sponsored by *Card Player* magazine. The thrust of my talk was to emphasize that those cardrooms which are successful are the ones that have good games and make an effort to do everything right, which assures that the games stay good. The talk began with the following statement in which I asked those in attendance to fill in the blanks.

I will enjoy my time in your poker room providing that

_____ _____ _____ _____.

I then presented some problems that I have observed in many cardrooms over the years. They are related to the responses I got to the above.

I. Dealers — Violation of procedures
1.   **The dealers pay attention.** The worse situations that I have ever observed at a poker table always occur because the dealer is not paying attention. What happens is that when the floorperson asks the dealer to explain the situation, the dealer explanation is not even close to the true events. This will frequently have the effect of infuriating all the players at the table, including those not involved in the hand. It is also a good way for a cardroom to lose some customers. Dealers

must be focused on the game at hand and must be aware of all action that takes place.

2. **The dealers deal at the proper speed.** Improper speed can be too slow as well as too fast. Slow dealers don't produce enough hands, and players generally like a fast paced game. Dealers who deal too fast tend to make more than an acceptable amount of errors.

3. **The dealers don't comment on the size of the pot or the play of the hand.**[15] Anytime a dealer (or anyone else for that matter) gives information that has the potential to affect the action, the game is hurt. In addition, when a dealer comments as to "What a big pot it is," he is usually looking for a toke. Needless to say, this will normally irritate the players and can sometimes even cause the cardroom to lose a customer.

4. **The dealers don't argue with the players.** Whenever a dealer has a problem with a player, he needs to immediately call a floorperson. Arguing will almost never accomplish anything except to irritate the player even more. This is true even if it is obvious that it is the player who is wrong.

5. **The dealers don't routinely expose cards.** In blackjack it is important that the dealers tilt the deck upwards. This is done to stop a dishonest player from "reading" the back of a card in case there is a mark on it. The problem with dealing this way in poker is that it can cause cards to flash. In blackjack it is not a problem. But in poker it is important that all down cards remain private. That is only the person for whom they are intended for should have knowledge of them.

6. **The dealers don't complain about lack of tips.** Dealers need to understand that those players who either don't tip or tip very little are still good for their income. Poor tippers still help keep the games going. If poker was restricted to only those players who are big tippers, I doubt if there would be enough players to sustain the games. A dealer should never

---

[15] Sometimes the dealer is required to state the number of players or the size of the pot.

complain about lack of tips. He must keep in mind that those players who tip little, especially if they are some of the regular customers, are allowing him to collect tips from those — frequently the tourist types — who are more generous.

7. **The dealers don't talk excessively — no extraneous talking.** I regard this as the most important problem on this list. Dealers who talk excessively tend not to be paying attention, are mistake prone, deal too slowly, and are simply bothersome to many players. When dealing, there should be no extraneous talking while in the box. A few cardrooms do a good job in this area. Unfortunately, many don't, and I consider it to be an industry wide problem.

8. **The dealer's don't chew gum, etc. while in the box.** I won't comment much on this except to say that a professional atmosphere goes hand-in-hand with good poker games. Chewing gum while in the box looks unprofessional to many. It may not seem like much, but it is the beginning of sloppy dealing which can lead to numerous other problems.

II Dealers — Common Sense

1. **The dealers don't call open seat immediately after a player goes broke instead of waiting until he is out of earshot.** Many people play poker simply because they find it fun. They love the action that it provides. Unfortunately, losing is not fun, but there must always be a loser. Because of this, it is important that the dealers be aware of the feelings of some of their customers. When a player goes broke, it is important that the dealer not remind him of this fact. It only takes a little courtesy to wait a few seconds before calling "Open seat." This could even be the difference between that player returning to play another time in your cardroom.

2. **The dealers handle occasional player abuse in a professional manner. (They don't try to discipline players themselves, but rather call a floorperson.)** This idea was actually mentioned above, but it never hurts to mention it

again. When there is a problem with a player it is not the dealer's job to do the disciplining. He needs to call a floorperson and keep the game moving. When the dealer gets too involved in this type of problem, he not only runs the risk of alienating the player in question, but he can slow down the game so much that he may upset the whole table.

3. **The dealers properly make change out of the pot.** This is only a problem in those cardrooms where the dealers do not carry their own tray. In these rooms, there is usually a limited amount of money in the tray. Thus, unless a dealer makes use of all resources, and this includes making change from the pot, many fills will be called for. This not only slows down the game, which the players don't like, but it reduces the house drop since less hands are dealt.

III. Management misconceptions

1. **Top cardroom management is highly visible on the floor.** It is my experience that those cardrooms where top management is never seen are the ones that get in trouble. Top management needs to spend time in their room watching the games and getting to know the players. Not only will this make management more aware of a cardroom's needs, it makes the players feel better since it will help them feel that management is on their side.

2. **Management realizes that the cardroom relies on winning players.** This is an incredibly important idea that many people in cardroom management fail to understand. A cardroom is very different from the rest of the casino. It needs winning players to be successful. These people help start games and keep games going. Without them, cardrooms would be hard pressed to have many games, and what games they have would certainly break down quickly.

3. **Management doesn't want everyone to break even.** This is a follow-up to the idea just stated. I have seen cardrooms where management restricts the size of the games, and discourages the tourists from playing in games where the

better players may be. Needless to say, this has the effect of lowering the "earn" of the potential regulars, even turning some of them into losers. Thus, on "off" nights the cardroom won't have the core of regulars to start games and keep them going.

4. **The cardroom has a well defined rail. (Poker games have difficulty surviving at those casinos where you must walk inside the cardroom to see the games.)** Poker games need to be seen. Those poker rooms which hide their games do not do a good job of attracting new customers. In rooms like The Mirage, which has a well defined rail where people can view the action, new customers are developed all the time. The idea that poker players like privacy is wrong. What poker players like is action, and "new blood" is a major source of action.

5. **Management does not tolerate known shot takers — cardroom management needs to talk to them.** Unfortunately, poker has a "grey area." That is some players who can get unethical aren't really cheating, but are still harmful to the game. An example would be those hold 'em players who buy a lot of chips and then hide their cards behind their chips in an effort to get players to act out of turn behind them. When this sort of thing happens on a continual basis, poker room management needs to address it. They need to explain to the offending player that cardroom management is trying to create good games, but that this can only be done with the cooperation of all regular players. If improvement does not quickly occur, it may be appropriate to discipline the offending player in other ways.

6. **Management does not overuse props.** I recognize that the use of props in many cardrooms is a necessary evil. When the core of regular players is not large enough to start games and keep the games going, proposition players may be an appropriate answer. However, since these are players who are trying to play professionally, they tend to promote "no action games," which are not the type of games that a cardroom

wants to create. It is true that many of your regular customers might play in a tight / no action fashion. But at least they are paying for the privilege to do so. They are not supplied by the house.

7. **Small buy-in tournaments that break-up games are not regularly scheduled.** Years ago I regularly played in a cardroom that would hold small buy-in tournaments that regularly broke up the game that I normally played. Not only did I find another room, but the offending room is no longer in business. I recognize that the very large clubs can hold small buy-in tournaments and not harm their games. I also recognize that these tournaments can be used as a promotional tool. But the medium size and smaller rooms need to be aware what affect these tournaments may have on their regular games.

Another problem with small buy-in tournaments is that they may attract undesirable customers to your casino. Several years ago I was in a major Las Vegas casino that had Frank Sinatra appearing in its showroom. I could tell by the way the people were dressed in the show line, that this was exactly the customers this casino wanted to attract. In the corner, the poker room was having a $12 buy-in tournament, and you could tell by the appearance of these people that this casino would not want them as customers. Needless to say, within six months that cardroom was closed.

8. **Games are not spread that are too close in size to other games.** Games which are spread that are too close in size to other games will have the effect of cannibalizing each other. It's true that a very large cardroom may have the player base to spread both $15-$30 and $20-$40 hold 'em, but very few rooms can afford this luxury. Rooms which start to do this will often discover that they don't have as many games as they used to. In addition, if starting a game close in limit causes another game to break, you may have some very unhappy customers on hand.

9. **Management does not promote pot limit and no limit games.**
   A. **Weak players almost never win.**
   B. **Cheating accusations are inevitable.**
   C. **Takes up a table that could be used for other games.**

Every cardroom that I have ever seen that promotes pot limit and/or no limit games on a regular basis has run into trouble. Many people recognize that these games upset the balance of luck and skill that poker needs to thrive. When weak players never have winning nights they will frequently quit playing — sometimes necessarily due to lack of funds — and the games will dry up.

But pot limit and no limit also causes a more sinister problem which very few people in the cardroom business understand. In a game where someone will occasionally lose all of their money because of the turn of a card, cheating accusations are inevitable. Yes, it is true that "one outers" and "runner-runner" do sometimes occur. But when a cardroom develops a reputation for cheating, whether justified or not, it is frequently just a matter of time before their business is damaged. I do recognize that if players come to a room on their own and request this type of game, that the cardroom should consider it, and I also believe that these forms of poker are appropriate side games for some tournaments. But again I want to reiterate, that in my opinion, it is a major mistake to promote these games on a regular basis.

10. **Poorly thought out promotions that attract undesirables players are not offered.**
    A. **Cheap tournaments.**
    B. **Money give-a-ways.**

Cheap tournaments and money give-a-ways can be successful promotional tools that a cardroom will want to use. But they need to be well thought out or you may find that the people you attract hurt your business more than it helps. Without being specific, promotions that pay people to play in small limit games will frequently have this affect. A promotion should strive to build on the strengths of the cardroom. This is frequently more important than merely bringing in additional bodies. This is especially true if those additional bodies have the effect of driving some of your regular players away.

11. **The tables on the rail are utilized efficiently — this is where middle limit games belong.** I recently walked into a cardroom where the only tables going were in the back of the room. The tables on the rail were empty. Needless to say, potential customers, who might be interested in playing if they could watch for a while were not attracted.

    It is also important which games are put on the rail. Small limit games aren't played for enough money to attract the interest of tourists who just might be standing near a cardroom. Very large games will attract their interest, but the amount of money at stake will often scare them away from playing. However, middle limit games are perfect. Games that use $5 chips, such as $20-$40 hold 'em have large enough pots to attract most people's interest, but are not so large that potential customers will not want to play. Cardrooms that put their smallest games on the rail and hide their middle limit games are making a mistake. The idea that their regular customers prefer "peace and quiet" as opposed to other casino noise is wrong. What they prefer are good games and attracting new players is almost always good for the games.

12. **An effort is always made to make sure that decisions are consistent.** I won't comment much on this except to say that it can be very difficult to achieve, and that all cardrooms should always strive for improvement in this area. I also recognize that there must be some flexibility in the decision making process. For instance, a questionable move made by

a cardroom regular may require a different decision than if it is made by an obvious cardroom novice.

13. **Management understands that a cardroom should not be like going to church. It will work with the regular players to achieve an appropriate code of conduct for a playing atmosphere (and this can include a minimal dress code).** Over the years I have heard and read numerous complaints concerning player behavior. In my opinion, player behavior is much better than some discussion indicates. But I do recognize there are times when it needs to be at a higher level.

On the other hand, when a cardroom sets down rules that are too strict in terms of behavior, they will not only take the fun out of poker, but they will probably slowly lose their business. Poker should be played in a relaxed atmosphere where some indiscretion is tolerated. If a major problem occurs, it should of course be addressed. The same is true for a recurring problem. But behavior rules that are too strict will be fatal for any cardroom's business in the long run.

14. **Newly hired dealers are not placed in the biggest games.** While dealing appears to be an easy job when a skillful dealer is in the box, it takes time to develop those skills. In addition, higher limit players are often more demanding than those who participate at the smaller limits, and the money on the table is frequently more meaningful to those in action. The solution to this is simple. Don't put break-in dealers in the biggest games. They should have some period of time dealing in the smaller games before they are moved up. This policy will not only be good for their dealing skills, but it will also be good for their confidence as well.

IV. Brush System

1. **New games are started with regard to those people already playing.** Nothing is more upsetting than to be playing in a game and have the cardroom start another game that causes your game to break, and you now find yourself

frozen out. This is especially true if you happen to be losing. The brush should always be aware of what calling down a new game will do to the current games. If it is likely to break a game that is already in progress, the best decision may be to put off calling down the new game.

2.   **The brush is not hard to find — potential customers enter and leave room.** When the brush is difficult to locate, the cardroom may lose some of its most desirable customers. The regular players will frequently wait around until the brush shows up, but someone new to poker will frequently leave. He will sometimes think that the cardroom just doesn't want his business. In addition, when this "new" money doesn't have a chance to sit down, it negatively affects the games since the marginal players will now have less opportunity to win and return on another night.

3.   **The brush does not discourage tourists from playing any particular game.** For poker to survive you not only need a core of regular players who start the games and keep the games going, but you also need some "live" money. When the brush tells an obviously weak player that a certain game may be too tough, he in effect assures that the regular players who frequent this game have a reduced "earn." In other words, he is contributing to the games not being good. It should be the brush's job to seat new players and inform them as to the length of the list. They should not be deciding who should or should not play in any particular game.

4.   **The brush pays attention to the games that have lost players thus assuring that the games do not break down when there is a live list.** It is a disaster to be playing in a game that breaks only to discover that there was a list for the game, but that the brush was not paying attention. When this happens, not only will you have some unhappy customers, but the overall drop of the cardroom is reduced. The brush always needs to pay attention to the games that he is attending. Failure to do so can cause many cardroom problems.

5.   **The brush does a good job of maintaining the transfer list.** There are many reasons why players want to transfer. It could be to find a better game, move away from a smoker, or just find a "lucky seat." But whatever the reason, players want the transfer list well maintained and coordinated by the brush. Failure to do so can result in some very unhappy customers, and sometimes they will have good reason to feel this way.

6.   **When a new game is called down, a dealer and chips are available.** One of the best ways to make your customers unhappy is to call down a new game and make your players wait for a dealer and chips. I have even seen situations where the dealer and chips were so slow in coming that by the time they showed up all the potential players had wandered off. Again, problems like this will only irritate many of your customers and hurt your business in the long run.

7.   **After a new game is called down, the game bank is picked up in an efficient manner so the game can get started.** Not picking up the game bank is essentially the same problem as above. Most players appreciate a fast paced game and getting started quickly is part of this process. When the brush neglects to pick up the game bank, causing the players and dealer to sit there, fun poker is not achieved.

8.   **After a new game is called and only a few players show up, the brush makes an effort to announce the game or check with other players on the list to see if they are interested in playing.** Nothing is more frustrating to a potential player than to go to a "new game" only to see that the brush makes no effort to fill the game. If there is a list, and the brush can check with some of the players on the list, he should do so. It might just be that the reason they didn't go to the new game was that they did not hear it called down. Again, when the brush neglects this responsibility, it will only have the result of irritating some of your customers.

9.   **When a player leaves a game to go to a new game that is being called down and the new game fails to go, the player can return to his old seat.** This is a problem that I have

personally complained about many times in many cardrooms. It is infuriating to go to a newly called game only to find that it doesn't go, and then to discover that your seat is taken and that you are frozen out. The brush needs to be aware where the players are coming from and not to fill their seats until he is sure that the new game will go.

10. **The brush does not over emphasize the high limit games.** There is no question that high limit games require more attention than the games at smaller limits. But the brush needs to be aware that he cannot sacrifice the other games just to satisfy the needs of these games. I do recognize that this is not always easy. But the brush needs to be aware that all players in the cardroom are important customers. Not just those who play in the biggest games.

To finish my talk I then provided the opening statement again with the appropriate answer and comment.

I will enjoy my time in your poker room providing that

<u>the games are good</u>.

However, if your cardroom suffers from some of the problems listed:

Don't expect the games to stay good.

Finally, I pointed out that whenever an adversarial relationship develops between players and cardroom management, the room is usually doomed. Once this adversarial relationship develops, it doesn't really matter whose fault it is. Cardroom management always needs to be aware of this, and when problems begin to develop they need to take appropriate action.

In the Cardrooms

Afterthought

Well, are the games good at the cardroom you play in? The answer should be yes. In fact, there is no excuse for the answer not being yes.

Cardrooms are always trying to increase their bottom line. Nothing wrong with that. But it is the way they try to do this that frequently causes problems. An emphasis on cheap promotions, cheap tournaments, and an over reliance on props is usually a strong indicator that something is wrong and that the cardroom is heading down the wrong path.

Put another way, poker management needs to emphasize running their business well on a day-to-day basis. This means good dealers, a good brush system, and a lot of common sense. This is the formula that will produce the good games all cardrooms need to thrive. It doesn't come easy, but with hard work it can be achieved.

Part Five

Hands to Talk About

Hands to Talk About

Introduction

Once you have read most of the good books and have a grasp of the important poker concepts, it's time to put it all together. Of course putting it all together isn't easy and it requires much thinking about the game both at and away from the table.

When an expert plays poker, he is able to make complex decisions accurately and quickly. This is absolutely essential to winning play. However, when someone relatively new to poker is faced with the same decisions, they often get completely lost and make costly mistakes.

So how do you go from making these expensive playing errors to expert play? In my opinion, the best way to do this is to try to work your way through the decision process for hands that are not necessarily straight forward. This brings us to some "Hands to Talk About."

Struggling With a King

Suppose we are sitting in a structured limit hold 'em game. It could be $10-$20 or $20-$40, or some other limit. You are two off the button, two players have limped in, and you hold

Should you play?

Clearly this is not a raising hand. In fact, in most situations it should be thrown away. The hand is fairly weak and many bad things can happen. But it becomes right to play under one circumstance. This would be when the rest of the players (including those in the blinds) are loose and passive. Now you would be getting the multiway action with little risk of a raise that this hand needs to be profitable.

But this alone does not make this situation worthwhile. You must be able to play the hand well, and that may include flopping top pair and then throwing it away. If you can't do this, having the above condition met is probably not enough.

Well, lets suppose the situation is right and you go ahead and call. Both players call behind you and both blinds call producing a seven player pot for one bet each. The flop now comes

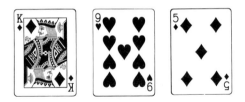

The two players in the blinds pass, the next player bets, the player on your immediate right folds, and now it is your turn. What should you do?

First, let's agree that if there was a lot of action before it got to you this hand should probably be thrown away. This could mean a bet and a couple of calls, or a bet and a raise. This is partly because there would be a good chance that you are already beat, and partly because if you did happen to hold the best hand, you could still be beat by the players behind you who have not yet acted, as well as drawn out on by those who don't yet have you beaten But this is not the situation here.

One thing you should be thinking about is how likely the bettor is to have a king in his hand. Many players, when they hold a high card and have the opportunity to be first in, will either raise or fold. They won't just call with this hand. You also need to think about whether this person will automatically bet a flush draw as many players do, and how likely he is to bet a hand like

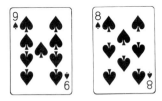

which would give him middle pair.

Let's assume that this analysis is favorable. If that's the case, you should raise and hope for the best. Part of the reason for this raise is that you think you may have the best hand and part of the reason is that you don't want to give someone with middle or bottom pair, or a gut shot, correct odds to call behind you. So you raise. Now say one of the players after you cold calls, the original bettor calls, everyone else folds, and the turn card is the

The original bettor now checks to you. What do you do?

First, let's agree that we don't like the fact that the player behind you called the two bets cold. He could be on a flush draw, but he can also easily have a better hand than what you are holding. This could be a king with a better kicker or a hand as strong as a set. But it can also be something that he shouldn't be playing. Many "live" players would make an incorrect call in this spot with something like an ace-eight hoping to get lucky. They feel that if they catch that ace or make three-of-a-kind they can gain three big bets from you and also collect additional money from the other player(s). However, they need a much bigger pot to make this call correct. Also, while it is true that if this player is on a flush draw, it makes it less likely that the initial bettor is on a flush draw, it certainly could be the case. That is they both could be drawing for diamonds.

Despite all the problems, your play is to bet. You just can't give a free card in this spot. (If you get raised [by either player] you will have to strongly consider laying your hand down. It is just not strong enough to continue unless you feel that there is a good chance that the raiser is making some sort of play.)

You bet and both players call. The river card is the jack of clubs making the board

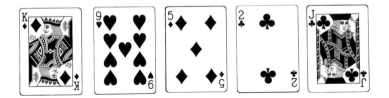

The first player checks to you. What should you do?

It should be clear to most of you that you should also check. The reason is not that your hand might not be best, but rather because it will be difficult for a weaker hand to call (unless you are against very poor players who will pay off with anything). If someone else bets, you should probably call unless you are very sure that this person hardly ever bluffs. There are now many bets in the pot and you don't want to be throwing away the best hand.

This ends our analysis. If you had trouble following all of it, your hold 'em game can probably use a little work. If you disagree with some of it, well there's always a chance that you are right and I'm the one in error. It doesn't take much to change the way a hand should be played, and in hold 'em it can sometimes be very difficult to decide upon the correct strategy. For instance, you might be able to make an argument for just calling on the flop and then raising on fourth street.

There is one point, however, that needs to be driven home. This was not a terribly difficult hand. Yet it required some sophisticated thinking. And if you want to be successful at the poker tables, it is this type of analysis that you will need to do all the time.

Some Logic Principles

When reading hands it is important to understand that your opponent should be playing logically. If he violates this precept, it is frequently a tip-off that all is not as it appears.

Of course, "logically" can vary based on the sophistication of your opponent. For instance, when playing hold 'em, if a typical player raises from an early position, it probably means that he has a good hand since he should be aware of his poor position. (This idea is also true in seven-card stud except that the other other upcards can influence the quality of a playable hand.) A more sophisticated player may know when it is proper to work in a few weaker hands so you can't be as sure as to how strong he is. A terrible player who is unaware of his position may raise with almost anything, and thus, become unreadable. However, his poor hand selection should more than make up for any advantage he gains by being tough to read.

The other night, while sitting in on a $15-30 hold 'em game, a hand came up that illustrated some of these "logic" principles. An early position player raised, the next few players passed to me; I held two aces and reraised, everyone else folded, and my opponent called. Thus, only the two of us took the flop, which was:

To my surprise, after the flop hit, my opponent bet. Now I had to decide what to do. Most players, I believe, would raise. They would conclude that with this flop their two aces is probably the best hand, and they would want to get more money in there with the best hand. A few players might be a little more tricky. They might just call on the flop, hoping to raise on the turn. Again they would conclude that their two aces is most likely the best hand and that this alternate strategy is probably the best way to maximize their profit. Very few players would consider anything else.

But there is something illogical about the way this hand was played and a good card reader would take that into account. It is the fact that in a heads-up pot, the person who made it three bets (before the flop) will bet virtually every time when his opponent checks to him on the flop, regardless what the cards on board are. A good card reader would immediately ask himself, "Why is my opponent not checking knowing that I will bet almost every time?"

Unless your opponent is fairly irrational, or exceptionally tricky, there are only two possible answers to this question:

1.   Your opponent has flopped a very strong hand, such as a set of jacks, and is looking for excess action.
2.   Your opponent is bluffing.

Notice that if the first case is true you don't want to raise since your raise will only cost you additional money instead of winning you a bigger pot. If the second case is true your raise will again cost you money. Now your opponent will fold instead of (possibly) bluffing until the end.

Thus, I just called my opponent's bet. A blank hit on fourth street, he bet and again I called. On the river a queen hit. He bet and I called once more. He turned over an ace-queen. My pair of aces won the pot, as my opponent had bluffed on both the flop and fourth street, and caught just enough to trap himself on the river. (If a non-helpful card came on fifth street I believe he would have bluffed again.)

Keep in mind, as this essay shows, that when your opponent violates an obviously logical play it may call for you to alter your strategy from what most players would believe to be correct. Of course there are always exceptions, but the ability to read hands and make the proper adjustments are some of the skills that separate the best players from the rest of the pack.

Finally, I want to point out that this advice applies best in heads-up situations. If one or more players had called behind me, it would probably be better to raise on either the flop or fourth street in an attempt to knock these other players out. Once the pot has become large it is now important to maximize your chances of winning it. The possibility of costing yourself an extra bet or two should no longer be an important component of your strategy.

A Pair of Fours

Perhaps the most famous hand I was ever involved with occurred in a $15-$30 hold 'em game at The Bellagio in late May of 1999. I thought the hand was interesting and casually posted it on one of our Internet forums. By the time the smoke cleared, the hand was all over the Internet, and there were several hundred posts discussing the pros and cons of my play. Because of this I thought that it would be worth repeating here, and give some of the reasons for my strategy. Here goes:

Four players had limped in and I had

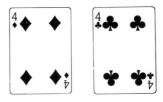

one off the button. I called, the player on the button raised, both blinds called, and all remaining players, including me, called. (Eight of us saw the flop for two bets each.)

The flop came

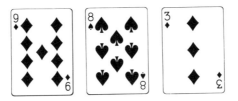

The player in the small blind bet, two players to his left called, I called, and the player on the button called.

The turn was the 3♠. It was checked to me and I bet. Only the player in the blind called. The Q♣ came on the river. We both checked and I won the pot with my two fours. (The player in the blind had A♦6♦.)

As innocuous as this hand might first appear, it stirred up a hornet's nest. Here are the reasons why I played as I did, plus some other comments.

First, it should be obvious to most readers that I am suppose to call before the flop with my pair of fours. I am simply getting enough multiway action to try to flop a set. (And calling the subsequent raise is of course a no brainer.)

My call on the flop is much more controversial. Generally, calling on the flop in a multiway pot with a pocket under pair is a mistake that only weak players make. But I felt that this situation was an exception since there were 19 (small) bets in the pot. It is only 22-to-1 for me to turn a set. There are 19 bets in there already, and if a four comes I could win as many as 35 bets, assuming my hand holds up. So at first this appears to be a very easy and profitable call. (However, note that if I did not hold the 4♦ my call would be wrong. This is because I don't want to turn a set at the same time someone else makes a flush since two diamonds flopped.)

But there is a problem. The before the flop raiser is behind me and if I knew that he would raise again it would cut my immediate odds down to 12-to-1 assuming everyone calls and no one else reraises. If this happens my call will become a mistake.

Nonetheless, it was still right to call. There are three reasons for this. First, the before the flop raiser doesn't have to raise again. Since my implied odds were overwhelming, it seemed like I had enough cushion to chance the raise. Second, if the player behind me raises again, he may just have two big cards and is trying to buy a free card. If this is the case and he succeeds, his raise has helped me as much as it has hurt me because I now get to look at fifth street for free and given that 12-to-1 is easily worth it. Third, his raise may tie on other players who may now be drawing close to dead assuming the four does come. So even though my immediate odds may drop, I may gain some extra bets which will partially counter balance this.

Well this call stirred up a firestorm. Some posters pointed out that I play terribly and am a known steamer. Others said that this was a highly fluctuating play which should be avoided or that the call could be made by an expert since he would be able to play the hand well enough to show a profit, while a typical player can't.

Let's answer these one at a time. First, whether I play badly or steam has nothing to do with whether the play was correct. Even terrible players or those on high tilt can accidentally make the right play, and even if the negative comments are true, there is no reason why my strategy can't still be correct.

Second, this is actually a low fluctuating play. The vast majority of the time I will put my money into the pot (on the flop) and throw my hand away on the turn. Occasionally I will win a big pot, and on very rare occasions I will hit my four and proceed to lose a few more bets. This is not what causes big swings to your bankroll.

(Straying from the subject a little, big swings are usually caused by hands like suited connectors. This is because you frequently flop a draw and then have to put a lot of money into the pot on both the flop and the turn in pursuit of completing it. Now you either win a lot or lose a lot, though you usually win more than you lose.)

Third, an expert player and a mediocre player should play this hand exactly the same. If a four comes you will either bet or raise, and if a four doesn't come you usually fold when someone else bets. There is very little "real" skill in your fourth street strategy.

But something totally unexpected happened on fourth street. The bottom card paired and there was no bet. When it was checked to me I realized that there was a chance I had the best hand and therefore betting was absolutely mandatory.

In fact, this is the key to my fourth street bet. If I do have the best hand, and with no bet to me there is a reasonable chance that this is the case, I must knock out every hand that might be drawing to beat me. Since anyone who stays will have at least 6 outs to my hand, I need to eliminate them.

The concept here is simple. *When the pot is very large, I must do everything possible to increase my chances of winning it.* For example, if one of the callers has a hand like K7 he has six outs to beat me. Since three people folded when I bet, I may have eliminated as many as 18 outs against me. (Note that if someone has better than six outs, such as a flush draw, they won't fold.) In addition, if I get someone to fold a hand like two fives (which beats me), I have just made a hugely profitable play.

Notice that there is almost no reason to bet on the end. If my remaining opponent has a better hand than I do, he will simply pay me off and I will just lose another bet. If his hand is worse than mine, he will simply fold and I gain nothing by betting the best hand.

Checking Aces

Here's an unusual play (for most people) I made with a pair of aces. It is another example of "correct," but uncommon strategy when the pot becomes large. I'll also give my reasons for making the plays that I did. It also needs to be pointed out that some of the decisions you are about to read are highly debatable, and if the parameters of the situation were changed just slightly, proper strategy may be quite different from what is presented below.

The game was $30-$60 hold 'em (played at the Bellagio). The blinds were $20 and $30, an early position player raised, a middle position player called, I held

and made it three bets. The player on the button called, the player in the big blind called, and the two players already in called. So far nothing unusual in my play. However it is a little unusual to get two cold callers for three bets each.

The flop came:

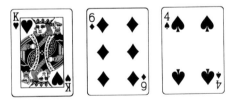

Everyone checked, including me. I suspect that most of you will think that this is crazy. Surely the two aces appear to be the best hand. But betting has its drawbacks. The problem with betting is

188

that there are 15⅔ bets already in the pot, and because of the size of the pot it is correct for many weak hands to call. This could even include a "pocket pair" because of additional bets that could be made on the later streets, in case the trip card comes on the turn. (Note: With 47 cards not accounted for, it is 45-to-2 or 22.5-to-1 that the pocket pair catches the trip card. Therefore, since you can expect to make some additional money if you hit your hand, a call should be correct. Exception: Your call might not be correct if one of your trip cards puts a possible flush on board. But that is not the case in this situation.)

But there is also another reason to check. Someone else might bet into you on fourth street with a weaker hand than your aces — and this could include an outright steal — and your subsequent raise might knock out a hand behind you which would have drawn out on the river. (For those of you who might be interested in these types of plays and when they are appropriate to make, see our book *Hold' em Poker for Advanced Players: 21ˢᵗ Century Edition*.)

The turn card was a complete blank. It was checked to me, I bet, the player on the button called, the player in the small blind raised, and the other two players folded. This raise created a dilemma for me since a likely hand for the raiser would be a set. However, it is also possible that my check on the flop would make him think that I had a hand like a pair of queens or jacks and would now bet, being less fearful of a king. If this was the case I could easily be against a hand like ace-king or king-queen which of course loses to a pair of aces. Furthermore, given the size of the pot it becomes important to reraise. This way I might be getting in more money with the best hand (against the turn raiser) and force the player behind me to fold, not giving him the opportunity to draw out on the river. This I did, and the player on the button folded and the player in the big blind called.

Another blank hit on the river and I checked after my lone remaining opponent checked. The reason for the check was that it seemed to me the most likely hand for my opponent was indeed a set, meaning that he would win the majority of the time that my bet is called. (Of course, a bet would have been forthcoming if an ace appeared.)

In fact, he did have the

and I won a very large pot.

Recapping, there are two plays in this hand that most of you would not make. They are the check on the flop and the reraise on the turn. Typical players would bet the flop, assuming they have the best hand, but only call the raise on the turn, being correctly fearful of being up against a set (or perhaps a hand like kings-up).

What they would not do is take into account the size of the pot. In fact, in most situations there is no question that betting the flop and just calling down are the correct plays. But sometimes when the pot gets big, correct strategy can call for some very strange plays. In my mind this was one of those situations, and I was fortunate to have my hand hold up.

Betting for Value

Here's another hand that I played recently. What's interesting about this hand is that, at first, it appears very simple, but there is actually a lot to it.

The game was $30-$60 hold 'em (with blinds of $20 and $30). I was two off the button, everyone passed to me, and I raised with:

Stopping right here, while there is no question that many players will automatically raise first in with this hand from a late position, it is clearly marginal in many situations, and probably unprofitable in at least a few others. For the raise to be optimal, you prefer for all remaining players to be "weak-tight." That is you want them to sometimes all fold, and to only rarely reraise. (This is particularly true of the player in the big blind.) If these players tend to be loose aggressive, or perhaps they play well after the flop, you should be much less inclined to make this raise, and instead throw your hand away.

Anyway, I felt my raising criteria was met and after my raise the player on the button called, and the player in the small blind called. Notice that having the player on the button only call does somewhat confirm my belief that the players behind me were weak. Almost all good players will either reraise or fold in this spot depending on their hand. Calling is an option that they will almost never consider.

So the three of us saw the flop which was

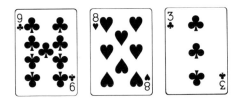

This is obviously a good flop for my hand. It should be clear to most of you that I did not have the best hand before the flop, but now my holding is top pair with a pretty good kicker, so there is a good chance that my hand is now best.

The player in the small blind checked, I bet my top pair, the player on the button raised, the small blind called both bets cold, and I called. There are two reason why my call is now proper strategy. First, after the raise and call, my chances of having the best hand have gone down. Second, even if I do have the best hand, many fourth street cards can beat it. This includes a third club, a card that can complete a straight, or an overcard (to my nine) that pairs a card in one of my opponents' hand. So by only calling (and not reraising) I can see what hits, and perhaps bet again if the card is favorable to me, or check and fold if a terrible card hits.

The turn was the K♣ which has to be one of the worst cards in the deck (for me). Not only does it complete a flush, but it puts a dreaded overcard on board, and since both of my opponents did call raises before the flop, it makes it a little more likely that a king is out. The player in the small blind checked, I checked, and the player on the button checked.

Everyone checking was somewhat surprising. While the player in the small blind might be checking a flush, it didn't make sense for the player on the button to do the same. He should also bet a pair of nines (or a pair of kings if the king hit him). Thus it appeared that he either raised me with a straight draw or perhaps something like a small or medium pair in his hand. He would be hoping that my hand was only two big cards and that the flop did not hit me, and that I bet automatically when the first player checked the flop.

The river was the 8♦ which put a pair of eights on board. The player in the small blind checked. His hand was now much more clear. He didn't have a flush, he probably didn't have a nine or king, and he certainly didn't have an eight (for three eights) since he would be very unlikely to call cold the flop raise with middle pair. His most likely hand was something like jack-ten giving him an open end straight draw after the flop. If I bet he would just throw his hand away.

However, the player behind me was a different story. If he had a nine, we would probably split the pot. If he had a pair in his hand I might get a call and win an extra bet. If he had an eight, it was going to be expensive.

This is where knowing your player can make a difference. Many players like to call raises with pocket pairs because they over value them in short handed situations, but are also unlikely to call raises with a hand like king-eight suited. When this is the case, you should bet for value a little more on the end than what at first might appear to be correct since your chances of being called by a weaker hand have gone up. That I did and when I turned my hand over my opponent threw his hand away.

In conclusion, I suspect that many of you will think that my strategy in this hand was not the best. There are certainly arguments to be made for folding before the flop, reraising on the flop, betting when that dreaded king of clubs hit on fourth street, and just checking on the river. In fact, the proper answer has something to do with not only how accurate your judgement is of your opponents, but also how you believe they perceive you. For example, if they perceive you as being very tight, you should be more inclined to raise before the flop. If they perceive you as an action player, you might be better off to muck your hand, watch the remaining players go at it, and wait for the next deal.

Over Playing the Ace-Queen

This time let's talk about a hold 'em hand I recently played in a $30-$60 game at the Bellagio. Again the blinds are $20 and $30.

The player under the gun raised. Normally this means that you will be looking at a very good hand as long as the player is at least moderately competent. It's true that he might sometimes try to run a weaker hand through, but this should not happen often enough to change proper strategy. However, in this situation it was a player known to be too loose and aggressive, but he is also an experienced player who is capable of playing his hands in a tricky manner.

I was on the button and held the

and everyone else had passed to me. Being aware that my opponent was too loose and too aggressive, my play was to reraise. I felt that it was correct to play the hand and wanted to get the pot heads up to maximize my chance of winning without improving.

In hold 'em, there are many situations where, if someone has raised, it is now your turn and no one else is in, and you are not in the blind, the proper play is to either reraise or fold. Why this is correct could easily be the subject of another essay, so I won't go into it here except to say that this was one of those spots. If I can't reraise folding is probably the proper play.

Anyway, after I made it three bets, the blinds folded and the initial raiser just called. However, I began to have second thoughts. I realized that my opponent was someone who could and frequently would play his hands in a tricky manner. Thus my situation was not as secure as it first appeared.

The flop was

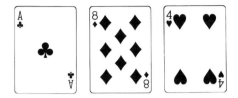

It was checked to me, and my bet was called.

At first this might seem that everything has worked out just fine. But that is not necessarily the case. Since my opponent does play his hands well once the flop comes, he should be aware that I have a strong hand since I had made it three bets (before the flop). Thus, for him to stay with me might be bad news for my holding. Furthermore, this was the type of player who would now slowplay a hand that could beat me (and go for a check raise on the turn) but should also throw away a weak hand.

The turn card was a deuce and we both checked. Based on the above, there were now two reasons to check. First, I might be beaten, and second, if I bet again and did hold the best hand, there was a good chance my opponent would now fold a mediocre hand since he would give me credit for having aces and had to face a bet on both the flop and the turn. Also notice that my check might induce a bet on the river with a hand that I could beat, but which my competitor would have folded if he had to call a bet on fourth street. Though my check might allow a miracle card to hit which could beat me, the same is also true for me in case my hand is second best. For example, if I am against an ace-king and would fold to a check-raise, by checking I might snag a queen which would then win me a nice pot.

Sure enough, just as I had hoped, a queen came on the river and my opponent bet. Here again I was in a tough spot. I could now be against a set of aces or queens, and if that was the case my hand would still be second best. On the other hand, two aces and two queens were both accounted for. This meant that there would still be eight possible combinations of ace-king left while only one possible combination of either two aces or two queens. Thus, if my opponent would only be betting if he held ace-king, ace-ace, or queen-queen I was still a 4-to-1 favorite. (Notice that this assumes he will always bet ace-king.) Thus, my play was to raise.

To my surprise, my competitor turned over his hand and showed that he had a pair of kings. He then thought for a short while before finally calling my bet, and I won a nice pot.

There are several conclusions that we can draw from this hand. First, even though it is good to play aggressively, sometimes, especially against better players, it is just better to fold. Even though I won a nice pot, it was probably best to just fold before the flop.

Second, just because you get a flop that looks favorable, it is not always right to bet, and there are other reasons to check than just slowplaying a big hand. Sometimes your check can save you some money if you are in a situation where you must call. Sometimes your check can induce a bluff. And sometimes, your "creative check" can confuse even someone who plays well and can win you additional bets on a later street (or in a later hand).

And finally, this hand also shows that there is a fair amount of luck (in the short term) in poker. It's true that the better players will win the money in the long run, but in the short term, anything can and sometimes will happen.

Trying For a Parlay and Then Some

I thought for this essay I would discuss a hand that David Sklansky observed in a $20-$40 hold 'em game that was played at The Mirage in Las Vegas. There were three players in the pot and the first player made several errors. All the players were considered regulars, but the first two tend to play a little too loose and too aggressive, while the last player is considered, by us, to be an expert.

The hand went down like this. The first player limped in from an early position, the second player who was on his immediate left raised, and the third player who was on the button called with the

The flop was the

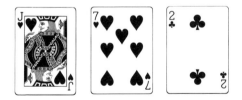

The first player checked, the before the flop raiser bet, the expert player (who had made top pair) raised, the first player called the raise cold, and the before the flop raiser called for one more bet.

A 3♦hit on fourth street. It was checked to the expert player who bet, the first player called, and the before the flop raiser folded. On the river, a ten of spades hit and the first player bet. He was called by the expert who won the pot, as the first player turned over, to everyone's surprise, a pair of eights.

Let's discuss the errors that this person made. First, let's agree that he probably played his hand correctly before the flop. Some players will routinely raise with a medium pair if first in up front, but in most games this is probably not correct since the main value of the hand with many players still to act is to flop a set.

His first error came on the flop. How can his call be correct? For it to be correct he would have to catch both of his opponents with hands like two overcards and a flush draw. That is he needs a parlay to occur.

Now what is interesting is that if he was against either one of these opponents in a heads up pot then he would be correct to call. This is simply because his chance of winning, given the size of the pot, is high enough to justify the call. However, just because he might be correct to call either player, it doesn't mean that he is correct to call both of them. This is because the probability that both of his opponents are out of line is roughly equivalent to the probability that the first opponent is out of line times the probability that the second person is out of line. This is a much smaller probability and it would require a very large pot to make the call correct.

A similar error is now made on fourth street. When a regular player calls a raise cold on the flop he is announcing that he has something. The expert on the button will know this and would be unlikely to bet again without a hand. This is because he knows that he will at the very least be called again by the first player because that player must have some kind of hand. Thus, it is again very unlikely that a pair of eights can be good on the turn.

The river play is a strange mistake which I occasionally see a "tourist" type player make. Obviously when the first player bets he is representing a hand like jacks and tens. For his bet to be correct one of two things must happen. He must either get his opponent to throw away some better hands, or get his opponent to call with some weaker ones.

It is very unlikely that either one of these will happen. If the expert does have a legitimate raising flop hand which almost always means (in this situation) a pair of jacks or better, he will call. On the other hand, if he really was out of line with something like a flush draw, he almost can't call. In fact, if you knew for sure that was his hand the correct play would be to check and try to pick off a bluff.

So how can a "regular" make this many errors in a hand? Well, just because someone plays all the time, it doesn't mean that they play well. I suspect that what happens is that some players don't spend any time analyzing the hands that they play. So even though they appear to be experienced, and have learned to play aggressively, they still won't win because they lack good fundamentals and have no idea how to read their opponent's hands.

A Few Decisions

The other night I played a hand in a $20-$40 hold 'em game that I thought would make an interesting essay. The reason for this is that I made a couple of unusual decisions which would be considered controversial at best, or just plain wrong at worst.

It was a late night action packed game. The following hand came up. A live player under the gun raised, an even "liver" player in middle position called, I held

so I reraised. The two players already in both called and no one else played. The pot was contested by the three of us.

The decision to three bet with the ace-king should be pretty automatic. First, there is a good chance that I have the best hand, and by keeping the pot to just the three of us, I will frequently win without improving. The idea that you should only call to see if you survive the flop is almost always wrong in this situation. By keeping it short handed you do not always have to hit the flop to win.

The flop came

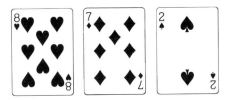

To my surprise the first player bet. The second player called, I raised. The first player reraised, the second player called both bets, and I called.

My thinking here was twofold. First, I am aware that after my showing much strength before the flop it could be very dangerous when the first player leads. He should know that I will automatically bet, so why does he lead? It appears that he is either completely out of line, possibly on a straight draw with a hand like ten-nine, or it is possible that he may have a very big hand. But I felt that I would have good control over this player. Even though he was fairly live, he did not seem overly aggressive and I thought that my raise would buy me a free card no matter what he held. Obviously I was wrong. Also his reraise probably means that he has either flopped a set, has an over pair, or has a hand like ace-eight (suited). However if he has an over pair it is probably not aces, kings, or queens or he would have made it four bets before the flop.

On fourth street an ace hit. The first player, to my surprise, checked, the second player checked, and I checked. This is clearly the most controversial play of the hand. When the first player checked I thought that if he had an overpair to the eights he might now fold even though he appeared fairly live. On the other hand if he made aces-up or had a set I would be (check) raised. Finally my check might get him to bet a weaker hand on the river.

The last card was a card that I was not real happy to see. It was another eight. The first player checked, the second (very live) player bet, I called, and the first player called. The second player (who had just bet) threw her hand away without even turning it over. I showed my ace-king and the first person then mucked his hand which confirmed to me that he had an overpair to the eight on the flop. It seemed that my fourth street check not only induced a bluff from the player in the middle, but it made the first person overcall.

It might seem that this hand was played brilliantly since I won a nice pot. But it was also fortunate that my hand was best. The question is did I really play this hand optimally, and would you play it the same way or employ a different strategy? For instance, my check on fourth street did allow a scary card to come off that easily could have bested my hand. (You may want to think about this before going on to the next essay.)

A Few More Decisions

Here's a "dream" hand that I recently played where the cards came just perfect. Although it would be profitable however I played it, decisions occurred that significantly impacted the amount of my profit.

It was a typical $20-$40 hold 'em game at The Mirage. Most of the players were playing too many hands and going too far with them. Other players did play a little tighter, but after the flop they did not play well. It was a moderately aggressive game.

(As an aside, I sometimes hear about how tough the games are in Las Vegas. In general the games at both The Mirage and The Bellagio — where I frequently can be found — are extremely good. If you play poker well, you should expect to do well in Las Vegas despite what you may occasionally be told. Of course,it is also true that if you play poker well you should have good results no matter where you are.)

Here's what happened. Before the flop the first three players called. A middle position player raised, and a late position player called. I was on the button with:

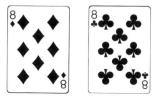

Clearly this holding is playable because it does well in a multi-way pot. But is this a cold call or reraise? The reasons to cold call are:

1. The value from flopping a set improves when I don't shut the blinds and early limpers out.

2.   If the flop should come small leaving me with the best hand, a late position bet would enable me to raise and knock other players out.

However, there are also some good reasons to reraise before the flop:

1.   It might not only knock the blinds out, but it might also knock out the original limpers. If I was sure that reraising would eliminate all of these players, then it would certainly be the correct play. This would produce a short-handed pot containing lots of dead money and give my two eights a better chance to win. However, most players in today's games will call the additional bets after they have limped in.

2.   Everyone may automatically check to me on the flop. Now if my hand does not improve to a set, I will have the option to see fourth street for free. Five percent of the time it will improve to three-of-a-kind on the next card.

Anyway, I decided to just call. In my opinion this is the play that most players would automatically make, but the fact is that it's a close decision.

The flop came

This was a great flop, but my hand was not invincible. Even though I have made my set, it could be against a made straight if anyone holds a ten-nine. In addition, there are many cards that can beat me. If the queen or jack pairs I could lose to a higher full house. Any club will probably make a flush. If a nine or a ten hits, someone will probably show me a gut-shot straight.

The action was as follows. There was a bet, a call, a raise, and a cold call before me. My choice was to either call or reraise. Normally, I try to build a big pot with a set. However, with this type of suited, uniform flop, and all the multi-way action, I felt it was best to call even though it's true that by calling the drawing hands are not being charged the maximum amount. But if the scare card comes on fourth street, I will frequently be glad I didn't raise. In addition, my reraise might knock out a hand like ace-jack or king-jack. Notice that these hands are drawing close to dead. Most players would have raised again with my hand. By just calling, however, I allowed five of us to see the turn card.

On fourth street the best possible card appeared. It was the 8♥. I now held the nuts and I could only lose if someone else held a higher set and also caught the perfect card on the river — two unlikely events. My job now is to make this pot as large as possible.

The betting was a surprise. It was checked around to the player on my immediate right who bet creating a dilemma for me. My hope was that the bet would come from an early position, that there would be several callers, and then I could raise. However, if I raised now I risked knocking out the other players.

I decided to just call, and two other players also called, creating a four-way pot. I believe that most players would have raised.

The river card was the 4♥, essentially a complete blank. This card should not have helped anyone. I still had the nuts but none of the draws got there. It was checked to me, which brings up the final interesting aspect of this hand.

Pausing for a moment, this hand interests me because of all the debatable decisions. But in poker there is one situation which can never be debated. When you hold the nuts, are last to act on the last betting round, and it is checked to you and you don't bet, there is something about poker you do not understand.

I bet, and two players called. There were some surprised looks when the other players saw I held quads without initiating any action.

Well, did I do a good job? I certainly won a big pot, but as previously stated it would have been a sizeable pot no matter what decisions I made. The question is "Did I manage to win the maximum?"

Hands to Talk About

Afterthought

Yes, reading hands is both an art and a science. It is also the major separator between the merely good players and the true experts, and it is the main reason why many only win a little, but a few win a lot.

But there is an aspect of reading hands that is very important, though rarely discussed. It is the ability to be flexible when it is appropriate to do so.

A good example of this was the essay "A Pair of Fours." When the hand was being discussed on the Internet, there were several posters who claimed to be good poker players, who argued that calling on the flop with an underpair must always be a losing play. But it wasn't in this case. It was clearly correct to stay in action.

Put another way, expert poker strategy requires constant adjustment. Sometimes the action and amount of money in the pot will require an unusual play. Other times you will need to go to an alternate strategy because it may appear that one or more of your opponents have adjusted to you.

In addition, as many of the essays show, small changes in your assumptions can dramatically change your conclusions which impact proper strategy. A simple example is that you should always fold against an opponent who virtually never bluffs when you can only beat a bluff. However, if this same person will fire occasionally with a busted hand and the pot is large, folding can be a mistake.

So in conclusion, I believe the best way to improve your poker is to always have a "hand to talk about." Most of you probably had difficulty following the many decisions which some of the hands required, but the experts can do all of this instantly at the tables. Part of the reason is that they have spent a great deal of time away from the table going over hands. Now when a tough situation comes up it is easy for them to recognize it and quickly apply the appropriate strategy.

Part Six

The Ciaffone Quiz

The Ciaffone Quiz

Introduction

There are many people writing about poker and giving "how to" advice. Unfortunately, most of this advice is mediocre at best, and as far as I can tell, a few of these so called experts hardly even play any poker.

But there are a few exceptions and one of them is Bob Ciaffone. Not only has he written several excellent books including *Omaha Poker, The Action Game* and *Improve Your Poker,* but he is well respected by his peers, and this includes many of the best players in the world, and is a force at the table whenever he sits down.

However, in a game as complex as limit hold 'em, not all experts will agree on everything. Sometimes the approach will be a little different, and sometimes the perceived value of a situation will differ, thus producing recommendations that vary somewhat depending on who is doing the talking and/or playing.

In 1998 Bob published a quiz in *Card Player* magazine that I thought was excellent and I'm going to repeat it here. Of course a few of my answers are different than his, but that's to be expected.

The Ciaffone Quiz

As just mentioned, here's Bob Ciaffone's limit hold 'em quiz. It is designed for what he calls a "mid-limit" $20-$40 game. I thought the quiz was excellent and since I have logged many hours over the years in hold 'em games of this size, I decided to also "take it."

1. You are on the button and no one has yet opened. What is the order of preference for hands with which to open with a raise?

A. Q♥T♥   B. A♠9♣   C. 9♦8♦

Answer: First: A♠9♣; Second: Q♥T♥; Third: 9♦8♦
This is also Ciaffone's order. However, he is hesitant about raising with the

and recommends folding unless the big blind is a tight player. I would raise with it almost every time. Part of the reason for this is that many players are too tight on the flop even though they defend loosely before the flop, and I might be able to steal once we look at three cards. However, if the players in the blinds are *very* loose, then a call rather than a fold can become correct.[16]

---

[16] See *Hold 'em Poker for Advanced Players: 21st Century Edition* for more discussion.

2. The game is ten handed and you are first to act. Which hands do you play?

A. A♠8♠   B. 66   C. K♥T♥

Answer: I play them all. Typical $20-$40 games almost always have enough multiway action to make all of these hands profitable. When the game gets more aggressive than usual I don't play the

and the

For me not to play the 66, the game also needs to be tight as well as aggressive.

Ciaffone says that all of these hands should be folded up front in a typical $20-$40 game in Nevada or California. Obviously I disagree. But I do concede that they are marginal hands and you need to be able to play them well to show a profit. If you are new to hold 'em and your "reading hands" skills are still improving and you don't yet do a good job of "anticipating the future" depending on what cards come, you probably should fold them. So for many of you, Ciaffone's advice is correct. If you are wrong to fold them, your long term loss will be small. Once you get a little more experience you can always add them in.

3. You are playing in a game in which the play has been straightforward. The pot is opened up front for a raise and the button makes it three bets. You are in the big blind. With which of these hands would you cap it at four bets?

A. A♥K♥   B. QQ   C. KK

Answer: It depends on how likely I think the initial raiser will now fold if I cap it. Most players, if they raise coming in, will automatically call for two more bets. When that is the case I will just call with two queens, but will strongly consider raising with the other two hands. If I believe that there is a good chance my four betting will cause the initial raiser to fold, and some weak tight players will do this, I then will probably raise again with all the hands with the possible exception of the kings.[17]

Ciaffone says he would cap it only with the kings. He points out that

1.   The extra bet won't usually get anyone out.
2.   When a solid player reraises an up-front raiser you need a very good hand to reraise.

As you can see, our answers, though not quite the same, are close.

---

[17] In Nevada cardrooms five bets is the cap.

4. The pot is four handed and unraised. You are in the big blind. The flop is

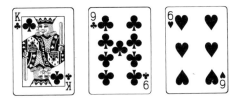

With which of these hands would you call a bet on your right?

A. K♠8♦   B. J♥T♥   C. T♦9♦

Answer: Ciaffone say none of the above, and I agree with that. I would probably raise with the

and throw the other two hands away. Ciaffone says to fold all of them. He points out that top pair with a weak kicker "is a dubious holding."

But is an eight kicker so bad in this spot? First, if the player in the small blind would have had a king with a big kicker he may have raised. Second, as we point out in *Hold 'em Poker for Advanced Players,* the chances of a king being out behind you has gone down since no one raised. And third, as Ciaffone points out a little later in this quiz, Kxx is a good flop to bluff at, and I will add to that a good flop to bet a hand that has some value but can't beat top pair.

This is a simple example of how card reading skills can lead you to a profitable play that other players who are "just trying to play tight" won't make. If you are throwing this hand away you are giving away too much. Now if this was no limit, then a fold would of course be correct. But in limit poker, there are often many other factors to consider than "If I play I may lose my whole stack."

By the way, you can also make a good argument for just calling with the K♠8♦ and I frequently will play it in this fashion. This way I can encourage someone who is bluffing or betting a weak hand to keep firing, and since there is only one overcard that worries me and the pot is fairly small, I don't object to someone "incorrectly" calling behind me.

5. The field of three other players in an unraised pot checks to you on the button. The texture of flop offering the best chance for a successful bluff is?

A. A-X-X   B. K-X-X   C. X-X-X

Answer: On this one Bob and I agree. K-X-X is the flop that offers the best chance of a successful steal. He correctly points out that too many people will play any ace and they are not afraid to check aces while X-X-X allows for someone to call with two overcards.

6. In limit hold 'em, position is most valuable with how many opponents?

A. One   B. Two or three   C. Four or five

Answer: On this one we again agree that two or three is best even though it is debatable in my mind. Bob points out that with more players you have to make the best hand to win the pot. Thus many of your poker skills won't come into play. With one player, while having position is certainly an advantage, the size of the pot dictates that position is not as important as when there are two or three players. There are some exceptions, but they are beyond the scope of this essay.

7. You are in the big blind. The flop is

A four handed pot is bet by the first player; you are second. With which hands do you raise?

A. J♠10♠   B. A♠9♠   C. Q♣J♣

Answer: I would usually raise with the A♠9♠ and usually just call with the other two hands. The reason for the raise is to narrow the field so that if an ace comes there is a good chance my hand will now be best. A secondary reason for raising is that my hand might beat the bettor, who may also have a draw, and I will be able to drive out middle or bottom pair. Now, if neither of us improves, I might win the pot.

   Ciaffone points out that with the

the nut flush draw, your hand is strong enough to raise, but that you do not want to knock out any straight draws or small flush draws, "so a simple call is the best action." Well I agree that your raise might knockout a gutshot draw, but I know of virtually no players who would throw away an open ended straight draw or a small flush draw. Not only that, if I held one of these hands I would certainly come for two bets. It's true that they are sometimes beat, but the pot, plus the additional money you expect to win if you make your hand, and it is good, is more than enough to keep playing.

The reason I would call with the

is that it is still a drawing hand and you would like to get more players. Since you hold a ten, it is less likely that another ten is out, so the secondary reason for raising that I gave above is not as strong. This is the hand that Ciaffone recommends to raise with for virtually the opposite reasons that I give to call. I cannot see why you would want to narrow the field with this hand.

By the way, if you were last with this hand you would certainly raise because it has so many ways to win. You can easily have 15 outs twice (to achieve the best hand). For this situation, even though it may not be "best" on the flop, there is a good chance that it is the hand with the highest "expectation."

As for the

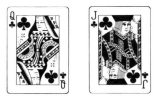

Ciaffone says that to raise with a flush draw on board is poor poker, and in this situation I agree. However, if your raise can get your opponent(s) to think that you are on a flush draw, it may still be worth it. Suppose your raise knocks the other two players out. Now a blank hits on fourth street and your opponent checks to you, you check. Now a spade that does you no good comes on the river. If you are against a player who can give you credit for a flush and fold his hand on the river when you bluff, then a raise on the flop makes sense. There are a few players out there like this and when I am against one of them I will raise most every time. However, you need to be very sure that your opponent fits this mode.

8. You are in the blind with the

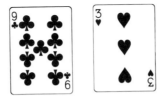

Two players call, so you are first in a three handed pot. The flop is all strangers:

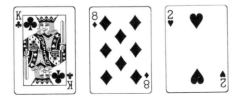

You check and the others also check. Fourth street is the innocuous 4♣. What percentage of the time would you bet out and try for a steal of the pot?

A. 25%-40% B. 55%-70% C. 85%-100%

Answer: On this one Bob and I agree. He says "If you steal only about one-third of the time here, you are winning only your "fair share" of the three handed pots. We aspire to win more than our 'fair share.'" The best answer is 55%-70% so that you won't be "too predictable."

Two more points. This is also a good flop to bluff on against only two opponents. Since no one raised (or else you wouldn't be playing the 9♣3♥) there is a good chance that no king is out. So while I agree with the bluffing percentage that Bob gives for fourth street, assuming there is no bet on the flop, I would have done some bluffing on the flop. I suspect that Bob would too.

The second point is that my bluffing percentage should be adjusted based on who I am against. Against certain opponents it might be right to never bluff, and against other opponents I might fire away almost every time. This is where paying attention to the other players in the game can really pay off.

9. Which of these statements about betting on the end are accurate?

A. A player who bluffs usually has busted, with no hope of winning a showdown.

B. A check-raise on the end is almost never a bluff.

C. Bluffing usually is done by a player while he is drawing rather than after he has missed, so most of the time, you should not call when holding only one pair when someone bets on the end.

Answer: First Bob says that A is true since a player with even a small pair is not nearly as likely to bluff as one with a "hopeless hand." I agree. In fact, this is the way that "you" should play. Once you have made a small pair, there are some hands, depending on the action, that you can now beat. Thus, there is no reason to risk a bet when all you can do is make someone throw away a weaker hand. An exception occurs against a player who is so live that he might call you with an ace, but sometimes get "inspired," and throws away a better hand. A few players like this exist, but notice that I said "a few." They are few and far between.

On B I agree and disagree with Bob. He points out that most players will bet out on the end because they are afraid that you won't bet, and thus, they will lose their chance to bluff. While this is generally true, I don't believe that it is always the case. Furthermore, in large pots, if you routinely lay down a "marginal" betting hand that gets checked raised, you may be giving up too much. Likewise, if you lay down too much, there are some observant players out there who will take advantage of your tendency to do this at a later time, and this can prove to be very costly to you in the long run. If it's wrong to call most of the time in these situations, because of the size of the pot, it can't be wrong by much, and I recommend that you don't "lay down" unless you are absolutely sure that you are correct.

By the way, you should also be playing in the manner just described. That is, if you discover someone who folds too much in this situation, fire away. The ability to be able to steal a bunch of big bets every now and then can add significantly to your long term profit.

On C I agree completely with Bob. He states "Stealing on the end is sufficiently common that you often are forced to call with a weak hand, because the pot odds are so high that you cannot afford to fold a hand that might win. Of course, it helps to know your players." This is very well said.

Note: In our books, and on our forums at www.twoplustwo. com, David Sklansky and I have been stressing that to become a top player, no matter what the game, you need to play your hands well all the way through. These three questions do a great job illustrating this point. Specifically, since we are talking about hold 'em, as you move up in limit and begin to play against better players, this area will become crucial to your success or failure. Most hold 'em players don't do a good job on the later streets. But the experts, who win more than their fair share of money, excel in this area. There are no exceptions.

10. Normally the maximum number of players you should try to bluff from first position is:

A. Three   B. Four   C. Five

Answer: This is a tough question, and Bob states that "Bluffing into more than three opponents is dangerous and very seldom succeeds." While this is generally good advice, especially on the end, I want to point out that there is a big difference between bluffing and semi-bluffing. For example, suppose I hold a hand like

in one of the blinds in an unraised multiway pot and the flop is

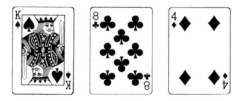

In this situation, betting into many players frequently makes sense. Notice that my hand is a gut shot (to the nuts), and if I check, there is a good chance that there will be almost enough money in the pot to make my call correct. Thus, if

there is only a small chance that my bluff will be successful, this bet can be well worth it. (See our books for more discussion.)

11. The winning style of play is:
A. Tight to start, tight with a large number of opponents, and aggressive in heads-up and three way pots.
B. Very solid at all times.
C. Highly aggressive. It is OK to contest a lot of pots if you are the one who is doing the betting.

Answer: Well, I don't think that you can accurately describe a winning style of play in a few words. I agree with Bob that B and C are not accurate, but I think that answer A over simplifies what an expert player does. For example, if you can knock out potential winning hands in large pots when you hold the current best, but not great hand, then you have gained a great deal. Notice that this will require aggressive play.

Also, playing tight with a large number of opponents is a common mistake that many poker players make. For example, advice such as, "You should throw your hand away if you don't have a least top pair in a multiway pot since you can't have the best hand" is clearly wrong. While it's true that you probably won't have the best hand, it can easily be right to call with bottom pair, weak kicker or even a three flush. It all depends on the size of the pot, the texture of the board, the players, the action, etc.

I would say that the winning style of play is to be able to understand hand values and how they change throughout a hand, read hands well, accurately project possible future action depending on what cards come, make plays that maximize your expectation, and much more. Now I agree that this will frequently produce a strategy that is "Tight to start, tight with a large number of opponents, and aggressive in heads-up and three way pots," but it will also sometimes produce a strategy that is very different from this.

To finish my comments on this question, Bob makes an unusual remark about former World Champion Stu Unger which I strongly disagree with. He says "You can try to play in style C like our current World Champion Stu Unger seems to do, but you are not going to get his results. It takes one heck of a poker player to play this way and not simply be throwing a party."[18]

Well this is an area that Bob and I have disagreed on before. What I am referring to is that I believe that Bob is getting no-limit and limit play mixed up. I only saw Stu Unger play limit hold 'em once in my life. (A game in which I sat in for a few minutes.) He surely played more than this, and there is no question that Stu Unger was a great poker player, but I doubt that he would have done very well in the limit hold 'em which this quiz addresses. It was not his game!

For years I have read from other writers, including Bob Ciaffone, that no-limit hold'em is much more difficult than the limit version. As is well known, I strongly disagree and have discussed this at length in my book, *Poker Essays.* But one thing is certain, I don't think it's fair to compare a no-limit expert's style of play to what we use in limit play. Limit hold 'em, as shown by my answers to this quiz, is an extremely complex game, and I believe that it is strategically much more complex than no-limit. This is why I emphasize how important it is to play your hand well all the way through. In no-limit, you frequently have all your money in or you just try to check it down.

I also believe that part of the reason that so many writers have jumped on the no limit bandwagon is that Doyle Brunson, in his book *Super/System,* essentially states this

---

[18] Stu Unger tragically died in his hotel room in 1999.

when he talks about the "mechanical nature" of limit and how no limit is the "Cadillac of poker games."

What may catch you by surprise is that I agree completely with what Doyle claimed. But there is an interesting reason for this. It is the fact that limit hold 'em, as played in our public cardrooms over a quarter a century ago, was structured differently and was not nearly as intricate as today's form is.

Specifically, the old game only had one small blind and the first person in could either call or raise only to the size of the current big blind. For example, a $10-$20 game had only one $5 blind and the first person in could just call for $5 or raise to $10. It was only after the $10 threshold was met could future bets and raises before the flop now be in $10 increments.

What this meant was that the old form of hold 'em wasn't really the same $10-$20 as we know today. The game was more like $5-$10-$20 and it produced much smaller pots. Now it was easier to bet enough to protect your hand, and proper strategy was much more mechanical and simpler.

The Ciaffone Quiz

Afterthought

I wish to thank my friend Bob Ciaffone for not only producing the quiz, but being a good sport about my answering it. Despite the fact that some of my answers are different from his, I want to point out that "The Coach" is extremely knowledgeable about all forms of poker and (as I mentioned earlier) is highly respected by many of the top players including those of us involved in Two Plus Two Publishing. In addition, for those of you who are interested in learning how to play "big bet" poker, the best book on the subject is *Pot-Limit and No-Limit Poker* by Bob Ciaffone and Stewart Rubin.

Part Seven

Two More Quizzes

Two More Quizzes

Introduction

Here are two quizzes that should do a pretty good job of testing your knowledge for both hold em and stud. Of course, even if you do well on the quizzes, it doesn't mean that you will have success at the tables, since knowledge is only one of the requirements for poker success. However, I can't imagine that if you understand the following material at the level of detail, presented, that you would do poorly in the games.

In any case, take your time with the questions and answers that follow and spend time thinking about those concepts that you either do not understand or disagree with. Also keep in mind that there is always some chance that I have a few things wrong, or at least the ideas may not totally apply to the games that you play in.

Hold 'em Quiz

Here's a short quiz on hold 'em. If you are able to get most of it right, and understand my answers at an appropriate level of detail, you are well on your way to being an excellent hold 'em player. If you struggle with the question and answers, you may need to work a little more on your game.

1. Suppose a player who plays far too many hands, raises, and you hold

Should you reraise?

Answer: You should put the third bet in only if this person *raises* with too many hands. Just because he *plays* too many hands, doesn't mean that it carries over to his raising requirement. In fact, many "live" players are still very selective in what hands they raise with. You'll see them limping in a lot and calling raises from others, but if they initiate the action with two bets an A♦Q♣ should hit the muck. This can be true even if the raise comes when they are first in from late position.

Ironically, if a good player raises first in late position and you are next with a hand like ace-queen, you should always reraise. This is because, in an effort to steal the blinds, he will expand his range of raising hands, and thus, become a "loose raiser." The live one, if he plays weakly, won't necessarily do this, and making it three bets can now be much more dangerous.

2. Why is a hand like ace-little suited better than king-little suited?

Answer: When most people answer this question they will quickly say that ace-little suited is better than king-little suited because you can make a higher flush. While that is certainly the case, it is not the main reason that Axs is better than Kxs.

So what is the main reason? It is that you will win more frequently when an ace hits on fourth or fifth street than a king. Catching your high card after you have flopped your draw is a significant part of the value of either hand.

Another interesting point is that sometimes you will need to raise to knock players out behind you to assure that all your outs are real. It is a disaster to catch your big pair (after flopping a draw) only to discover that a player behind you has made the same big pair and takes down the pot.

3. Suppose you raise with a hand like a pair of jacks, you get one or two callers, and then a late position player reraises. Now the flop comes all small cards. Should you lead or go for a check-raise to avoid giving the players in the middle a free card?

Answer: You should do neither. Notice that the player who reraised before the flop will almost always either have you beat or will have two overcards to your hand. If he has you beat, you certainly don't want to lead or check raise the flop. If he has two overcards, and you check, he will almost always bet when the action gets to him, and if you (or someone else) bets, he will almost always call. Thus, the overcard which you would like to keep out, in case your hand is good, will be there anyway. This means that in a case like this, it is almost always right to merely check and call the flop.

4. Suppose you hold a hand like

or

are in late position, and a couple of players have limped in. What is important to consider when deciding to make a call?

Answer: You need to consider how well your opponents, particularly the first player in, play. This is because, when good players limp from early positions, they frequently hold hands like

or

Now it is easy for you to make a second best hand which will usually cost additional bets.

In addition, if the first player in is someone who likes to limp with big hands, such as aces or kings and then reraise, you should also fold, even if he doesn't play very well. On the other hands, if these are people who play many hands, you should take advantage of your good position and play the marginal holdings. Just be aware that they are only slightly profitable, and if you have doubt about playing them, it will never be a major mistake to fold.

5. Suppose you have either a pair of kings or a pair of tens, you raise first in and get two callers behind you. The flop comes

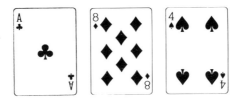

With which of these two hands is it much more important to bet?

> **Answer:** The pair of tens. Not betting here can dramatically impact your chances of winning. If no one has an ace, checking now lets a king, queen, or jack drop off that can beat you.

If you hold the kings, notice that none of these cards are very threatening. So not betting will have very little impact on your chances of having the best hand. In fact, if there is no ace, your allowing a card to drop off may make someone a second best hand and gain you additional bets. So you can see that the strategy of always betting in this spot, which many players follow, is clearly wrong.

6. Suppose you have started with two aces and are last to act on the flop, which appears to be non-scary, and there are several players in. When is it correct to check your hand if everyone checks to you?

Answer: The time to consider making this unconventional play is when the pot is very large. If you bet, as most people would, anyone who has a piece of the flop, such as bottom pair or a gut-shot, will call and be correct to do so, given the size of the pot (assuming that your hand is best.)

On fourth street, they will call again after everyone has checked to you, and you again bet. Notice that these players will have opportunities to draw out on you on both the turn and the river.

However, if you check your hand on the flop, there is a good chance that someone will bet into you on fourth street, and you can now raise. This will frequently allow you to collect extra money from someone whom you have beat (and might even be bluffing), and to force out other players taking away their chance of drawing out on the river.

The downside of this strange play is that the fourth street card that you let drop off might make a miracle hand or a decent draw for someone who would have folded to your bet. For instance, if a deuce comes on the turn it could make someone a set who would not have played for one more bet. However, despite the downside to this strategy, when the pot gets very large, it can be right to make this strange play.

7. **Suppose you are playing heads-up against a very aggressive player, and to assure that he doesn't steal too much, you have determined that it is correct to play against him 60 percent of the time when you are in the big blind. A third player sits down. Now suppose he raises, your new "friend" folds on the button, and you are left in the big blind. (Assume only one big blind.) Do you still play six times out of ten?**

> **Answer:** No. The reason you played so much was to thwart your opponent's aggressive strategy. However, all that needs to be done now is for either of you to thwart his aggressive strategy. That is, the calling burden is now shared by both of you.
>
> However, you should still play much more than the player on the button. This is because it costs him twice as much as you to call.

8. **You are on the button with:**

Everyone passes to the player two seats to your right who raises. The next player calls and you make a debatable reraise. Unfortunately, the player in the big blind makes it four bets (after the small blind folds) and the other two players both call. Furthermore, you know that the player in the big blind will only make this play if he has a very big pair. Do you just call, hoping to flop a set and then folding if a nine doesn't come, or do you make it five bets (in those places which allow it), thereby often getting to see fourth street for free if the nine fails to show?

Answer: First notice that if you don't cap the betting, the player in the blind will bet and it is unlikely that either opponent will raise because of the perceived strength of his hand; and the fact that most players will wait until fourth street to raise in case they have made something exceptionally strong. So you will have the option to see the turn card for five bets anyway.

However, what if you make it five bets (before the flop) and you do flop a set? Wouldn't you prefer that the first person in be betting, instead of having everyone check to you? The answer is that in almost all cases you are much better off for someone else to be leading and this is more likely to occur if you do not cap it. Thus, it should be clear that this is the best strategy.

9. Before the flop, five or six players limp in, including a non-expert who plays regularly in one of the blinds. The flop comes

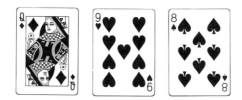

The non-expert checks, a player behind him bets, another calls, a late position player raises, and now our non-expert makes it three bets. What is his hand?

Answer: This is a simple hand reading exercise that incorporates the way the hand was played with the tendencies that an unsophisticated player would have. We could not be as sure if this same hand was played by an expert, since he might cross us up, usually dependent on his view of his opponents, and not hold a hand totally consistent with his betting. But with aggressive, unsophisticated players, this will usually not be the case.

First notice that to make it three bets, our hero must have something of value. However, also notice that forcing the first two players to call two more bets makes it difficult for them to call, and our non-expert should know this since he is a regular player. If he held a very strong hand, such as a set or a straight, he wouldn't be so anxious to knock people out. So it appears that he has a medium strength hand that will have a better chance of holding up against a smaller number of players. Expect to see something like bottom two pair or a hand like queen-ten, which produces both top pair with a questionable kicker and a gut-shot draw.

10. Suppose you raise before the flop with a hand like

and are called by a player in one of the blinds. The flop comes ace high and looks good for your hand, but to your surprise the player in the blind bets out. How should you proceed?

Answer: First notice that your opponent's bet is highly suspect since it should be clear that you will bet automatically given that it is just the two of you in the pot. This usually means one of two things. Your opponent either has you badly beat and is looking for extra bets, or you have him badly beat and he is just taking a shot at the pot.

In either case it should be obvious to you that you don't want to raise. If you do hold the worst hand, your raise will only cost you additional bets. But if your opponent is taking a shot, your raise can still prove expensive since it will signal him to fold his hand. By only calling he may keep firing through the river and you may gain two double size bets.

11. Suppose you are on the button and hold

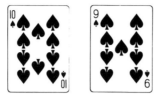

The player on your immediate right has just entered the game and has posted a late position blind. Everyone has passed to him and he raises. What is your play?

> **Answer:** First notice that correct strategy for the player with the late position blind is to almost always raise. Part of the reason for this is that in poker there are many situations where either folding or raising is a better option than just calling. Because of the late position and the additional money in the pot from the blind, this is one of those situations. Therefore, since the player on your right can't fold, unless he is very inexperienced, he should, and will, frequently raise.
>
> Now this brings us to your hand. Given that the player on your immediate right can have almost anything, a ten-nine suited is too strong to fold. And guess what? Raising has to be a better play than calling. For if your opponent flops a weak hand, which will frequently be the case because he may be starting very weak, he will be forced to check the flop and fold to your bet. (Your reraise allowed you to take control.)

12. Suppose you start with a hand like:

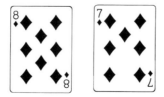

and flop a four flush (with two cards to come). Since it is now approximately 2-to-1 that you make your flush, does this mean that you need at least two opponents to make a flop call profitable?

Answer: No. In fact you can almost always continue on against one player. The reason for this is that there is additional money already in the pot from the first betting round, plus the fact that if you hit your hand, you may be able to collect additional bets on either fourth or fifth street.

Now the above is probably obvious to almost everyone who reads these questions. But it is still important because it is a very simple example of an error that is very common among intermediate players. And that error is not taking into account the size of the pot.

What happens is that someone will realize that he is beat, with only a small chance of winning, and quickly folds. But gut-shots do occasionally get there and bottom pairs sometimes do improve to the best hands. In large pots these are often worth a call, and unless the pot is extremely small, a four flush should not be folded.

13. When you flop a legitimate draw, either a four flush or an open end straight, but there is a pair on board, should you fold?

Answer: It is rarely, if ever, correct to fold. You must take into account the size of the pot. It is true that it is approximately 2-to-1 to make your hand. Nonetheless, you will occasionally run into a full house. Thus, to continue you need to get a little better than 2-to-1 to make your call profitable.

However, in today's modern structured games you will usually be doing far better than 2-to-1. In fact, winning ten or more bets when you complete your draw is not uncommon, so folding can only rarely be correct.

14. On fourth street, if you bet and are raised, and you cannot beat (and have little chance of outdrawing) a legitimate raising hand, should you fold?

> **Answer:** It very often depends on who you are against. Against a weak player you should probably almost always fold. This is because he won't make the raise unless he really does have it.
>
> But against an aggressive player, folding automatically can be a big mistake. That's because on fourth street they will frequently raise with currently weak hands that have the potential to improve. This includes holdings like middle pair that have now picked up a gut-shot straight draw or a flush draw that has added straight potential. Making automatic laydowns against this type of player can be a big mistake

15. Suppose you are on the button and you hold

Several players have limped in and you know that if you raise, everyone will automatically "check to the raise." Is this a reason to raise or just call?

> **Answer:** The answer to this is that it probably depends on exactly how many is several. If several means three or four opponents, then you probably like the idea that everyone will check to you. Now if you flop top pair, which will be the best hand, you will be able to bet, and if you don't hit your hand, you have an option to take a free card. If an ace or a queen comes on the turn, there is a good chance your hand will be best.

But now suppose you have seven opponents. First, if you make top pair, assuming your hand is best, you would certainly want someone betting into you so that your raise can knock others out. When you bet after it is checked to you, anyone with anything at all will be getting proper odds to call.

Second, what happens if you take a free card, assuming that you don't flop anything. Now the situation is not as good as before, since if an ace or queen comes on the turn, it can easily make someone else two pair, given the number of opponents you have. This is especially true with the ace.

So what is the conclusion of this? It is that when your opponents are always willing to check to the raiser, it may not be such a good thing if you happen to be that raiser. Of course, there is much more to consider than the number of players that you will be against when deciding to raise or just call with a hand like A♥Q♣, but it is definitely a factor.

16. Which hand has more value, a medium suited connector or a small pair?

Answer: To answer this question you have to understand how these hands play. They are very different and collect money in different ways.

First, let's look at the small pair. It's main value is in flopping a set. Otherwise you will usually fold them. But what you want are opponents who are willing to put many bets in the pot once the flop comes. This translates to aggressive players.

But how does a suited connector do against aggressive players? Now the situation is much different, since unlike a set, you only rarely flop a completed hand. But you do frequently flop a draw, which aggressive players will make you pay to make. Furthermore, they will sometimes bet you out of the pot when you make something like a gut-shot or a pair and three flush.

So this should answer your question. Even though both hands prefer multiway action, the small pair does better against moderately aggressive opponents and the suited connector does better against more passive ones.

17. In which game should you play more hands, one that is loose and passive, or one that is tight and passive?

Answer: As David Sklansky and I point out in *Hold 'em Poker for Advanced Players*, loose/tight affects the mix of hands that you play, while passive/aggressive affects the number of hands that you play. When most people think in terms of loose versus tight, they are more often than not thinking in terms of loose and passive versus tight and aggressive; you certainly should be playing less hands when the game is tight and aggressive. Let's look at a couple of examples that pertain to the two game types addressed in the question.

Suppose you are dealt

in early position. If the game is loose and passive, this hand becomes playable since you can expect:
1.   To get the multiway action that the hand requires, and
2.   Will probably only have to put in one bet assuring your good implied odds

If the game is tight and passive, the second condition will probably be met, but the first condition won't. In addition, if anyone does come in behind you they will probably have a much better hand, while in the first game type this wouldn't necessarily be the case. So we can see that 8♠7♠ can be played up front if the game is loose and passive, but not tight and passive.

Now let's suppose you hold:

are three positions off the button, and only the blinds are active. (This can easily happen in a loose and passive game if a couple of players are walking and/or terrible hands are out up front.) In the loose, passive game you should just fold. For, even if you raise, you are too likely to get players behind you and at least one of the blinds will always play. This means that to get a positive return on your money you will almost always need a very good flop, and that won't happen enough with this hand.

But what if the game was tight and passive? Now there are two ways to win. If you raise, everyone might fold, or if you get callers you may still be able to win it on the flop (or later in the hand). This swings the Q♣T♠ to a playable hand.

Thus, we see that both loose and passive games, and tight and passive games do present the opportunity to play additional hands. This means that you should play roughly the same number of hands in either game, but that the mix of hands will be different. Of course, whether a particular hand is playable or not will depend on the exact situation and the particular players that you are against.

18. When you are playing short handed, are in the big blind, and are against an aggressive raiser, what must you do?

Answer: Call frequently. The reason for this should be obvious. If you don't call a fair amount out of the big blind, your aggressive opponent will show a profit by simply raising nearly every time. Thus, you must get in there to thwart this strategy.

Now, many players do intuitively understand this and they do call a fair amount before the flop. But where they err is that they don't carry this idea over to the next round. Here again, (because of the size of the pot) your opponent has a profitable bet if you don't call enough. That's why in *Hold 'em Poker for Advanced Players* we recommend that you often ignore the top card on the flop, and then make your calling decision. If you were to only call every time you flop a pair (or better), a draw, or overcards, you will not be in there enough.

19. If you flop top pair in a multiway pot, should you usually lead if you think your hand is best?

Answer: The answer depends on whether you want people to call with weak hands, given exactly what your hand is. If the pot is small — no raise before the flop — you usually want them to do this. But when the pot is large, their calls will frequently be correct, and now your desire to make sure that no one gets a free card may not be the best strategy. In these situations you should often go for a check raise, and if there is no bet or the bet comes from the wrong spot, you want to consider going for a check raise again on the turn.

20. Suppose you start with a hand like:

You raise and everyone passes to the player in the big blind who holds

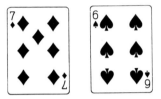

Do you want him to play? What if there were several other people in the pot; would this change your decision?

Answer: If you raise (without a big pair) and everyone passes to the player in the big blind, you almost always want him to fold when he has two cards unrelated to your hand. The reason for this is that he will out flop you approximately one-third of the time, and in most games he will be getting 3½-to-1 from the pot.

(Note: This doesn't mean that you should automatically call a legitimate raiser out of the big blind when you hold a connecting hand and no one else is in. Not only does he have position on you, but he can easily hold an overpair to your cards.)

However, the situation reverses once several other players are in. He will still out flop you one-third of the time, but now you don't care, because if your hand doesn't improve, someone else will usually out flop you if he fails to do so.

On the other hand, if an ace or a queen does come, he will only have a "two card flop" to work with, and he will have to hit the board twice to beat you. So now you want him in. In other words you now only care how often he will beat you those times when you flop at least a pair, which is not very often.

Seven-Card Stud Quiz

Here's some questions and answers for seven-card stud. Like the hold 'em quiz, the answers are detailed and fairly complex. If you do a good job on what follows, it is fair to say that you are probably well on your way towards expert play. If you struggle with them, and are confused by some of the answers, you have your work cut out for you. (This quiz refers to games where the ante is fairly large. In most cardrooms this means $15-$30 or higher.)

1. If you start with a pair of aces would you prefer that one of your aces be up or that your pair be concealed?

Answer: Almost every beginning player will tell that you want your aces concealed. This seems like the obvious answer, and there are certainly some advantages having them down. But there are many spots where you would actually prefer to have them up. If your aces are concealed, it will be obvious that you probably have the aces (or at least a large over pair) and now your kicker is known.

For example, suppose a player with a king up raises and you felt that a likely hand for him in this spot is a pair of kings. You are next with a small card up and you reraise. You are telling him that you have aces in the hole, and if you make two pair (or trips) by sixth street, he will always know this.

So it turns out that when your opponent knows your kicker, he gets a significant playing advantage. If he knew that you had aces but didn't know your kicker, he should fold, but now he should play.

By the way, this is certainly a reason to occasionally reraise someone in a similar spot when you don't have aces (or an appropriate big pair in the hole). A live ace-high three flush now might do the trick. This play can be especially good when it is much more doubtful that your opponent has the hand that he is representing.

2. Suppose you start with a big pair and have one opponent who starts with a medium card up. On fourth street you catch a blank, but he catches a straight flush card. What is your play?

> **Answer:** Your play is to check and call even if you think you have the best hand. There are basically two reasons for this. They are:
>
> 1. If you check, the money will almost always go in there anyway.
> 2. By betting, the only hands your opponent will fold are hands that you would want him to play.

This second idea is very important in seven-card stud and comes up in many other situations. Because of the draw out nature of one stud hand versus another, it is often right to chase, especially if the ante is reasonably large, with hands that appear relatively weak. But this doesn't mean that it is correct to chase every hand.

For instance, if you bet, your opponent might throw away a hand like:

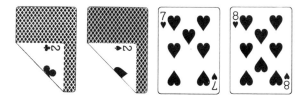

which he perhaps played hoping to just get lucky on fourth street. By betting he might just fold, but by checking, he will be inclined to bet, representing a stronger hand than he really has and you will theoretically make money. (Now instead of getting lucky, he got unlucky.)

3. You are dealt:

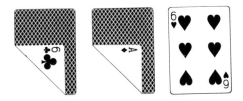

Do you prefer to play against one opponent or several?

Answer: Most inexperienced players will say that they prefer to play this hand against many opponents. This way if they catch another six or make aces up they will have many players to collect from. But that's not quite the way that stud works. That's because the most likely way that you improve this hand is to two pair, and that two pair doesn't have to be aces-up.

In addition, against many players, aces-up isn't necessarily a strong hand. In fact, in many spots it is little better than a pay off hand. A more mathematical way of putting this is that the probability of winning if you improve to aces-up is going down faster than the pot is going up.

On the other hand, what happens if you are against only one player? Here, most of your wins will come when you make two pair, and many of these two pair hands will not involve a pair of aces. Of course, having an ace in your hand tips the scale to those times that aces-up does beat something like kings-up or queens-up, thus you need it to make the play profitable.

The bottom line of all this is that a hand like a small pair with an ace kicker where your cards are live, actually prefers to be heads-up. This sometimes means that you should reraise to get it that way.

4. You have started with a big pair and have led on the first three betting rounds. On sixth street you are still unimproved, still have three opponents, but have no reason to believe that someone else has made a better hand. Should you bet again?

> **Answer:** There's an interesting idea that comes into play, which David Sklansky has called the "Horse Race Concept." It is the idea that with a medium strength hand against multiple opponents, you can be a favorite against each opponent, but still be a money dog to win the pot. Thus, there are many spots in which a bet on sixth street is wrong with this type of hand.
>
> Of course there are exceptions. One of them is if you think your bet might get one or more of your opponents to fold. If this is the case, your probability of winning the pot has gone up, and in large pots like we are describing here, that can make a bet well worth while.
>
> Another time that you should bet is if your hand has some other potential. This can be something as little as a gut-shot straight draw or just very live cards. Now the underlying probability distribution of the horse race concept is changed, and your bet can show a profit.

5. Why is it important to frequently take a likely second best hand and try to knock out a third best hand?

> **Answer:** Stud is often called a game of knocking people out and in many situations this is a very accurate description. This goes back to an idea that has already been mentioned. It is simply that, when heads-up, it is very easy to beat a better (starting) hand if you only improve a little, but very difficult to win the pot with this same amount of improvement against multiple opponents. Therefore it is often correct to take a second best hand and knock out a third best hand.
>
> Here's a simple example. Suppose on third street you start with a small three flush in a multiway pot. Notice that

this is precisely the situation that you want to be in with this hand. On fourth street you catch a card that looks like a blank to your opponents, but it also makes you a small pair. The player on your immediate right, who is representing a probable big pair is high, and as expected, comes out betting. Since your hand is too good to throw away, you should be willing to raise and knock the other players out unless someone behind you has caught a threatening card.

By the way, even though we have been saying that you should be willing to knock a third best hand out when you are only second best, it can be even better if you reverse the situation and knock the second best hand out when you are third best. Furthermore, even though the example given was for a fourth street play, this idea is important no matter what betting round it is.

6. When playing heads-up, which hand is better:

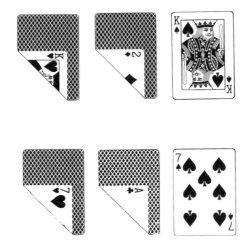

or

Answer: This is an idea that I have discussed in my writings before and the answer is probably not what you would expect. First, if you do a "hot and cold" simulation where the cards are dealt out over and over again it will show that the pair of kings will win about 58 percent of the time.

So at first it appears that the kings is substantially better. In fact, if each player was to close their eyes and put a bet in on each street, the split sevens with the ace would only be slightly profitable in games with large antes. But fortunately, that isn't the way stud (and all poker for that matter) is played.

What happens is that the player holding the split sevens has many playing advantages over his opponent with the split kings. This includes being able to act last, being able to fold when an open pair appears on board, and sometimes getting play when he pairs his door card.

All of this has the effect of making the hands much more similar in strength. So I'm not sure which is the better hand heads-up. The pair of kings will certainly win more pots, but the two hands should roughly split the money.

7. When you play against a big pair on third street, why is it important to have an overcard if you hold a small pair?

Answer: We have already mentioned this, but let's look at it in a little more detail. Suppose you compare

to

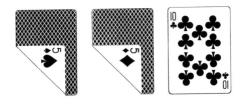

We know from above that the bigger pair is the favorite. If you were to deal all the cards out, you would see that the pair of fives would only win approximately 36 percent of the time, and even with the playing advantages that we looked at above, this would not be enough to make this hand profitable, heads-up, unless the ante was incredibly large.

But what happens if we switch the T♣ to the A♣? Now the pair of fives will win approximately 43 percent of the time which makes the hand profitable. The ability to make aces-up makes a difference, even though many of the wins for the pair of fives do occur when small two pair is made. So having that big overcard kicker does make a difference.

By the way, a straight flush kicker can also make a difference. For example, if we change the T♣ into a 6♦ the pair of fives would now win approximately 40 percent of the time. This might be enough to play as an ante steal where the 5♠ 5♦T♣ would not be, or it could make it correct to play against a high card raiser where there is some doubt that he might not have a strong a hand as he is representing.

8. If you have a hand that you plan to play on third street, what criteria makes it a raising or reraising hand?

Answer: One characteristic of stud games, once you get to $15-$30 or higher, is that the ante is a significant factor in your strategy. Being able to win it or being able to theoretically own a significant portion of it is very important.

Also, many hands don't have the potential to make "big hands," but they can easily make a medium strength hand.

What this means is that you should raise or reraise with many hands, if the raise has the potential to increase the chances of your winning the pot by about 20 percent. (With a very high ante the percentage doesn't need to be this high.) This can include hands like three high cards, a small pair with a large kicker, and a three flush with a high card. Notice that at first, some of these hands don't necessarily look like raising or reraising hands. But, when making these plays, be sure that your hand is live.

9. A player raises with a queen up and you are behind him with

Do you reraise?

Answer: There are basically two reasons for reraising with this hand on third street. They are:
1. To get more money in the pot when you think you have the best hand.
2. To knock other players out and play heads-up against a likely smaller pair.

Now suppose the likely pair of queens raises and there are still several players to act behind you. Notice that both conditions are met and you would certainly want to reraise.

But suppose you are last to act with only the bring-in behind you (who will likely fold). Now the second condition is not met and the value of your reraise has gone down. So the question that now needs to be asked is are there any advantages to not reraising since the pot will usually be heads-up anyway?

Well, the answer is yes. And it is not only the fact you gain deception, it is also the fact that only calling the raise might help you on future hands where it would be correct to only call even though a king was your upcard. Now your opponent(s) may be suspicious that you have that pair of kings again and play their hands incorrectly against you, given that your hand is something completely different.

10. Several people have limped in and you hold:

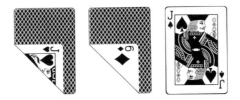

Should you raise?

Answer: Even if it appears that you have the best starting hand, the answer is still frequently no. The reason for this is simple. You don't have a hand that plays well in multiway pots. Thus, even though you may be starting with the best pair, stud is a seven card game (as its name implies) and you don't want to invest a lot of money with a hand that might not have much chance of winning.

What you usually want to do is to see what happens on fourth and fifth street. If the cards come bad, it will be easier to get away from the smaller pot. If the cards come good, your opponents may not suspect your hand is a big pair and you might be able to get in one of those raises that will knock players out.

By the way, an exception to this is if you feel your third street raise will cause one or more of your opponents to fold.

This fact can make a big difference in your strategy. But most players will not fold if they have limped in, no matter how weak their hand might be.

11. Now suppose your hand is:

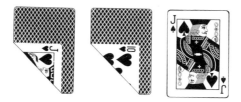

and several players have already limped in. Should you raise?

Answer: There is a big difference between this hand and the previous one. It is that your kicker is now a straight flush card which gives your hand much additional value, especially in a multiway pot. You should raise virtually every time.

Experienced hold 'em players will immediately know why this raise is correct. It's for the same reason that you usually want to raise after many people have limped in and you hold a hand like:

12. On sixth street, you will sometimes find yourself in a situation where you are either a small favorite or a huge dog. When this is the case, what is your best strategy?

Answer: You should check and call. Hold 'em players might be inclined to bet and then fold if raised, but stud doesn't work that way since the hands are harder to read and there could be more intermediate hands for your opponent to raise with.

Here's an example. Suppose you have an unimproved big pair that you have been betting all the way. You're not sure whether your opponent has been calling you down with a smaller pair or was just on a flush draw which he may have now completed. If you bet, you will frequently be raised and have to call, since you might be raised by a pair and a four flush, or perhaps small two pair. As with many other stud situations, if you check, the money will often go in their anyway.

13. Why are there fewer maniacs at the stud tables than at the hold 'em tables?

Answer: Seven-card stud is a very different game from Texas hold 'em and this is one of the places where the difference is readily apparent. In hold 'em, there is a great deal of luck between the first two betting rounds, where the number of cards goes from two to five. This means that getting out of line with certain types of hands, particularly if first in, is not necessarily penalized that much. Thus, the game can produce a large number of maniacs. They usually don't win in the long run, but they can certainly last a long time.

In stud, most of the luck occurs on the later betting rounds where the number of combinations increases at a higher rate. For example, with six cards, there are six possible five card hands, but with seven cards, there are 21 possible five card hands. This means that players who get out of line on the early rounds, which is where the maniac wants to operate, are severely penalized at the stud table.

14. What is the most important factor in seven-card stud?

Answer: It is the liveness of your cards. Even if you don't master many of the important poker skills and don't understand many of the meaningful concepts in stud, if you play fairly tight and make sure that your hands are live, I believe that you can survive in most games.

Let's look at an example. Earlier we saw that 7♥A♣7♠ would win approximately 42 percent of the time against K♥2♦K♠. But that was assuming that all cards were live. If you removed one seven from the deck, the percentage would be close to 37 percent. If both sevens are taken out of the deck, the winning chances are now reduced to 32 percent. Yes, indiscriminately not playing live hands can make a big difference. It can easily turn you from a winner to a loser.

15. Suppose three pairs clash in a three way pot, but the smallest of the pairs has a large overcard kicker to either of the other two pairs. Who is worse off?

Answer: Lets look at an example of a three way confrontation. Suppose the first hand is:

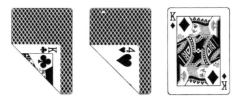

The second hand is:

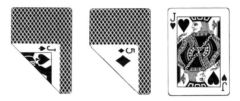

and the third hand is:

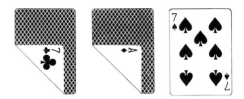

In a three way confrontation, the approximate results are 42 percent for the pair of kings, 26 percent for the pair of jacks, and 32 percent for the pair of sevens. Notice that the ace not only makes a difference, but that it really hurts the pair of jacks. This means that when a situation develops such as a jack raising in early position, indicating a probable pair of jacks, and a king reraising indicating a probable pair of kings, and you have a live hand that contains a small pair with an ace kicker you should "jump the fence" and get in there.

16. Why is it very dangerous when your opponent pairs his door card on an early round?

Answer: The obvious reason is that he may now have three of a kind which is a very tough hand to overcome, plus it can be very expensive to try. And, in my experience, they will show you a set about half the time if you play the hand all the way through.

But what most people don't realize is that the other half of the time when they don't make a set, they can still have a fairly good hand. This can be two pair or something like a pair and a three flush. Thus, if you start with a big pair, you will discover that sometimes you are a big dog — this corresponds to them having a set, sometimes you are a small dog — this corresponds to them having two pair, and sometimes you are only a small favorite — this corresponds to them holding a hand like a pair and a three flush. But the bottom line is that you are on average in big trouble, even though there is some chance you have the best hand.

17. When playing stud, we have put much emphasis on playing live hands. But suppose your *opponent's* hand is partially dead. How does that affect your playing decisions?

Answer: Just as it's important to play live hands, it is also very important to be aware if any of your opponent's cards are dead. Earlier we saw that the 6♦5♦5♠ would win around 40 percent of the time against Q♥4♦Q♠. But if we were to take a queen out of the deck, the percentage moves up to almost 45 percent. Now the pair of fives is clearly worth playing, and to assure that you get it heads-up, you may want to reraise. This would be true even if you were very sure that you are against a pair of queens.

18. What is a hidden factor when making your stud decisions?

Answer: It is how the hand will be played, which is usually a function of your opponent(s). However, there are many other factors that can come into play. This includes what the upcards are, how many players are in, the order to act of each player, and so on.

Here's an example. Suppose the pot is raised and then called; you have a three flush, but two of your flush cards are also out. In other words you have a close decision. The deciding factor could easily be the player in the middle. If this is someone who will quickly raise with a second best hand on a later street, you may want to lean towards folding. If, on the other hand, this player is not aware of this concept, and is also the type that gets "married" to his hand, it becomes correct to call.

19. When playing short handed against loose aggressive players, what is something you must do?

Answer: You must occasionally splash around. This means that you must sometimes raise with hands that hardly seem to be worth a call in order to stop your opponent from getting too large an edge from his semi-bluffs.

Here's an example. Suppose you have a small card in the door, but have a pair of sixes in the hole and have caught weak cards on both fourth and fifth street. Your opponent, who has also started with a small upcard, has now caught two overcards to your pair, is high on board, and bets into you. Your play will be to occasionally raise. If you have caught your opponent with no pair, he may fold immediately, and given the strength of your hand, you want him to do so. In a full game, a play like this would only rarely be correct, since it is so much more likely for your opponent to have started with a legitimate hand.

20. How do stud boards affect proper strategy?

Answer: In stud it is important to understand that the higher board is in many ways in control of the hand. This means that the person who is first to act will often do the initial betting, and it means that you can sometimes represent board strength to make your opponent fold when you want him to do so. An obvious example would be when you have a four flush showing on sixth street but in reality have a very weak hand.

But there is also another side to this story. It also means that you should frequently not bet when your opponent checks his better board into you. A common place for this is on fifth street when your opponent catches a big card like an ace or a king and then checks. If you bet and he folds, you probably wanted him to stay in the pot. If he calls and your hand is best you have probably only earned a fraction of a bet. But if you bet and he raises, you have cost yourself a lot.

Two More Quizzes

Afterthought

If you have done well on either quiz, you are definitely on your way to becoming a very good player, if you aren't already there. Of course, having the knowledge doesn't mean that you play well yet. You now need to be able to put this information to work and make accurate decisions at the poker tables. Here, there is no substitute for experience and thinking about the game. Combining these attributes with appropriate knowledge is what makes a strong player.

Notice that in the paragraph above I said "Done well on either quiz." My guess is that while only a few people will have the ability to do well on one quiz, a much smaller amount will do well on both of them. But in my opinion, that is what all good players should strive for. I have seen too many stud games which were very good, sitting next to tough hold 'em games because the hold 'em experts didn't play stud. I have also seen the opposite.

Conclusion

One day over twenty years ago I had a very strange conversation when playing low limit draw poker in one of the now extinct cardrooms of Gardena, California. A retired recreational player, who was sitting on my right, leaned towards me and began to articulate that poker chips were actually made from old cheese. "After the cheese gets very hard," he explained, "they punch holes in it and then paint these pieces producing the different denominations..."

Of course this story was ridiculous. But what's really interesting is that I have heard and read many ridiculous proclamations concerning poker. It seems that many players live in a world of make believe and it shows in their play and in their results.

Why so many players are like this is not entirely clear, but one thing is for certain — that's the way it is. It is also why poker games have been good for a long time and continue to be that way. People latch on to inaccurate ideas and just won't let them go despite their poor results.

Along these lines there is a player I know who is at best a marginal winner. When he has stepped up to $30-$60 (or higher) he has not had success. What's interesting about him is that he likes to discuss poker problems and won't yield from his opinions. This is true even when he debates players who are far more successful than himself.

So this brings us to the final words of this book. *Poker is a game of constant adjustment.* Yes, you have to play solid, which sometimes means that your style will appear boring and straight-forward. But you also need to play your hands well all the way through. You can only do this with a complete understanding of the concepts that govern strategic play, and the ability to balance and adjust these ideas as the game progresses. This takes a lot of work and dedication, but it is a whole lot better and much more fun than punching holes in old cheese.

Index